THE BUDDHA'S NOSE

One Man's Journey through an Imperfect Life

by

Ted Heaton

The Buddha's Nose

For information address: info@mickiedaltonfoundation.com

First Published in 2014 in Australia

ISBN: 978-0-9923422-3-4

PRINTED IN AUSTRALIA
Revised First Edition

Published by The Mickie Dalton Foundation
Kempsey, NSW
Australia

www.mickiedaltonfoundation.com

Acknowledgements

I need to acknowledge many people, but I'll make it short: my wife Toni,; many of my past students who years ago continually beseeched me to write this book; Damien Howard for bringing Buddha and his nose into my life in reality; to my daughter Taryn who I constantly learn from and is a great advocate for goodness and truth; and Michael Davies my teacher of all things written, as well as my editor, mentor and friend.

In addition a special loving thought to the spirit and memory of my son Ted Jr and his creative art work, some of which graces these pages.

Thank you all so much.

Dedications

I dedicate this book with the deepest possible love and respect to Toni, my wife emeritus, who, year after year, has shown me true love, care and understanding and has never stood in my way to be myself, regardless...

About the Author

Ted Heaton has been interested in human behaviour since well before Socrates drank the hemlock.

He has retired a number of times in his life, once as an international insurance executive, once as a college Dean and a few times as a psychotherapist. He has led a well and truly diversified life …. International Vice President and speaker in Insurance marketing, President of a Super League ice hockey team in Australia, a teacher of conversational English in Hong Kong, President of a Chamber of Commerce and Industry, President of a Far East direct marketing company, ghost buster and researcher of psychic phenomena.

Ted has lived in five countries, worked in many more, always searching for answers to life. He holds a number of qualifications including a PhD in Esoteric Psychology and has been a contributing author to various magazines and journals in America and Australia over the past 40 years.

He can be reached at: tedheaton32@gmail.com

Table of Contents

Coming Soon.....

Foreword

This book is not intended to be a lecture or class on Ancient Wisdom or Metaphysics.....I've done all of that for well over four decades. It's not intended to be an autobiography, although it has to sound like one, with most of the juicy bits missing, but it's actually aimed at the male of the species and is about sharing ways and means I improved my life as a man, by taking advantage of the issues and circumstances I have found myself in over more than eighty years on this crazy, mixed up planet.....being presented with simple but effective ways and means to develop self enlightenment.....reaching out for personal authenticity, reducing overbearing negativity, increasing positive thinking and letting the soul shine through the garbage that is there blocking it.

Once I found out that I had a "Core" somewhere I started the search for personal enlightenment. In metaphysical terms that 'search' is called 'The Path' and I'm still on it and will be till I shuffle off this mortal coil. In the meantime, the self-imposed therapy that this book directs me toward is often quite scary but I already know that the process of writing will finally reach a state of finding the real me and you can do the same.

Frankly, there's no bullshit here; just what is and was.

I'm writing this *mano-a-mano* for two reasons: one, to maybe make life easier for guys out there that have been hurt, have hurt others, are hurting now or might get hurt because of who and what they are, and what they've done that pisses them and others, off.....especially others: two, to help me cleanse my soul and prepare for the next life, whenever, whatever and wherever that might be.....and maybe pay off some karmic debt while I'm at it.

What has helped me is that I learned many years ago, what intellects such as Roberto Assagioli, Douglas Baker, HP

Blavatsky and others already knew and taught me; *that we are not human beings learning to be spiritual, we are spiritual beings learning to be human.* Understanding and accepting that rule changes everything that goes before it! Think hard about that.

The world is the canvas on which by example I will paint the meaning of my life. My body is the frame that for now I wrap around my soul.

Levels of Consciousness

Throughout the book many references will be made to various levels of consciousness. For this reason I want to describe them to the reader right up front so there will be no surprises when conscious-type issues arise.

I believe that we need to explore the various levels of consciousness in the human that are responsible for the generation of dreams because the more we explore and understand our levels of consciousness, the more effective we will be as we search for the Authentic Self ... the *real* us. Dreams are a primary source in helping us peel away the unknown or misunderstood aspects of who and what we are.

The wonderful philosophy of Huna was able to deal with three of the five levels of consciousness with amazing simplicity and clarity when they stated that there was the High Self, the Middle Self and the Low Self, end of report.

The High Self is the Super Conscious, Soul or God in us.

The Middle Self is the Conscious part of us that we are on now as you read this section and consider its validity; it's the awareness in us.

The Low Self is the Subconscious where 80% of our behaviour resides, often without us even being aware of its existence or influence on our activities and thoughts. I call the Low Self 'George.' He has a tendency to act like a kid most of the time....he accepts fixed behaviours, or engrams from Authority Figures without question usually and is often childlike in his thinking and living. He's not good or bad, he just is.

In addition to the three selves there are two more levels of consciousness, actually unconsciousness. The ancients called them Akashic Records but Carl Jung (a closet esoteric) changed all that when he renamed them the Personal Unconscious and the Collective Unconscious.

The Personal Unconscious is the collection of all the aspects that are you, now and in the past, both genetically and through past life experiences.

The Collective Unconscious is that part of you that is a member of the Human race and shares energies with all people on a collective basis. You easily see this play out in crowds and groups of people gathered such as sporting or musical events, times like Diana's death, the holocaust, the universal love of mother or Muhammad Ali. Regardless of colour, creed, the place on Earth where they live the feelings and sensations are the same, they are Collective.

The Buddha's Nose

Introduction

Just as the 2013 month of December broke gently over the current calendar site at the beautiful, humid, ocean-side city of Darwin, my good friend Damien surprised us with a very special pre-Christmas gift.

Over the years Damien has been to Bali perhaps dozens of times and during his excursions there, one of the things (there are certainly others) he is always anxious to attend to is singling out available new types of Buddhas to bring back to his home in Darwin, where many, many now reside, inside, outside in the gardens, and around his pool. For him, Toni my wife, and me, there is strong impact in the Buddha's energies and meanings. As psychologists, active or retired, we consider the Buddha to represent the concept of enlightenment--- of reaching for personal authenticity... or *wabi-sabi* in Japanese thinking.

One early morning as Toni swept the living room drapes back to let the new tropical sun pour through, which was soon beating a seasoned path to the nearest air conditioner, there on our veranda was the bust of a beautifully carved stone Buddha. When I say 'bust,' it wasn't quite. I mean the head was there and it was attached to the neck and a couple of inches of the chest area. Damien had found a way to deliver it to us without us even knowing it was there. It was a heavy puppy too...he'd have struggled.

What was remarkable was that the face had a unique expression of countenance given to it by a nose that was slightly, but noticeably, chipped. It looked character-building to me, maybe because I have a nose something like that myself, and I'm a character, some people tell me. But soon I could see a deeper meaning; it indicated the imperfections that so many of us go through life challenged by, some of which we deal with successfully, and some we don't....*wabi-sabi.*

Toni and I tried to lift the bust and take it to the back yard near the pool, but we couldn't....it was too heavy. Eventually John, our next door neighbour and I did the deed. Once it was set in place it occurred to me that the struggle we had getting it there was similar to life: some things are too tough at first, but perseverance can win out. I'm looking at it now, as I write this. Although his eyes are closed, I swear he's smiling at me, a smile of contentment and peace! The more I look, the broader the smile. I wonder if I should give him a nickname to make him more personalized. I'll think about that.

I've thought about that, it's **IRVING.**

And so the reason for this book was born, not just an addition to the ever-growing level of bibliotherapies that are out there, but hopefully it's intended to be of use for those who seek answers to the questions that permeate their very being: where fear is the bully and resolve, the solution. The Enlightened One....Wabi-sabi...a chance to become authentic with yourself and others....the ultimate journey. The Buddha's Nose promises results providing you can see the possibilities and will take the responsibility of making things happen.

Remember, *it's not over till the Fat Lady sings*.

As I recall it in the 1960s in Philadelphia Kate Smith, a top entertainer of the day, with abundant girth, was hired to sing God Bless America before the start of the Flyers hockey games at home. The team soon noticed that when she sang the song they usually won the game and, hockey players being superstitious by nature, kept her on in that capacity. At the time she was known as The First Lady of Radio. Fans and teammates both began to feel that when she sang the song they would win the game and it was all over red rover for the opposition. Fans began to chant "it ain't *begun* till the fat lady sings." Today the New York Yankees baseball team play her recording of God Bless America at every home game at the seventh inning stretch and the superstition survives. She was an institution. While through the years the message has changed slightly from 'begun' to 'over' its power hasn't and now "**it's not *over* till the Fat Lady sings**" has international status and meaning.

The Buddha's Nose

The Buddha

Here's a flash for you.....the Buddha was a MAN, just like you and me, brother. His energy is the basis of this book, as you'll soon see; not the religion involved, just the energy of personal enlightenment and development. So I thought I'd set the stage with an intro to the Buddha himself. This is the story...............

Gautama, Prince of Kapilavasta, was an Aryan Hindu who lived about 500 years before Christ. He succeeded the previous Buddha, Kasyapa, as Head of the Second Ray of Love Wisdom in the Occult Hierarchy of this planet. According to traditional ancient teachings eons ago, there were two brothers who shared their knowledge of the occult and stood equal in their development: one was known as the Lord Buddha, and the other was the Lord Maitreya, later known as Jesus of Nazareth. Many incarnations later our present Buddha, who is the fifth of seven that will appear, took his form as Gautama and lived, worked and preached for most of his eighty years of life.

He drew around him all of those who had been his pupils in previous lives. Before that existence he had been the Egyptian Hermes, and later walked among the Greeks as Orpheus, where he did his main teaching by means of music and song. His presence and power grew mightily throughout the world when he was considered by the Chinese to be the hero Mayadevi, and was born of a virgin. Story sound familiar?

The Buddha's Nose

Upon reaching the highest initiation, the Lord Gautama immediately made himself available to undertake additional spiritual development, which he practiced in each lifetime since his ordination. And with each life came special virtues of immense qualities that were meant to help his fellow men by teaching them the Wisdom that is eternal. He also undertook to return to this world once each year, on the anniversary of his last physical death and to take that special time to flood the world with his blessing. This time of blessing is a unique and marvellous expression of his love for us all.

Each May, at the precise moment of the full moon he appears to celebrate the most momentous occasion of his last incarnation...namely his birth, his Buddhahood, and his death, or "departure." This annual event of great magnitude is called in Indian "Vaisakh," and in the Ceylon language it is referred to as Wesak, or the Wesak Festival.

Those that have seen the apparition all describe it identically as a wondrous event that presents itself as a human form surrounded by an incredible aura of concentric spheres of glorious colours. The aura of the Buddha permeates the entire planet and is magnified in its intensity by the enormous number of groups of believers around the world who use the exact time to meditate as deeply and spiritually as possible. Through that channel they become part of the Buddha's aura and by doing so receive his blessings while they spread the message of peace, love and contentment throughout the earth. And the channels of Enlightenment are at their maximum expansion over a period of about thirty minutes. The Lord Maitreya, or the Christ, joins with the Buddha at the Wesak Festival to provide the combination of the powers of enlightenment and wisdom (Buddha) and love (Jesus).

Besides the Wesak Festival, there is one other period in the year that has particular significance and that is the full moon of July, a time known as the Asala Festival. This is the time when the Buddha's teaching to his five disciples was handed down and has come to be known as The Four Noble Truths and the Noble Eightfold Path, or The Turning of the Wheel of the Law. The sermon that the Buddha presented was *"**Choose The Middle Way.**".....the life of asceticism on the one hand and the life of materialism on the other, with the need of balance between the two lives in all matters.........the absolute need for moderation in all things good and the removal of negativity....to be aware of our Mind, Body and Power....and to live within the Law of Karma.*

His sermon proposed these points:

Right Belief....
Right Thought....
Right Speech....
Right Action.....
Right Means of Livelihood.....
Right Endeavour.....
Right Memory.....
Right Concentration.

The Buddha's Nose

It is this Noble Eightfold Path that the Buddha taught his followers was the spiritual value of Enlightenment....or as he put it, *"**To Know Thyself and Return to Your Beginning.**"*

For students of Ancient Wisdom, a Buddha is one whose higher principles have nothing more to learn, or be added to, in this manvantara or realm of humanity, on the earthly plane of existence. He/She has reached the state of Nirvana, or super-spiritual state of "heaven" and beyond. He/She has won all and gained all!

A Buddha of Compassion is a Man or Woman who has lived the sacrifices that go with abandoning all that is mean, wrong, selfish, ignoble, arrogant, thoughtless and self righteous, and by allowing the Light imprisoned within to kindle the sparks that turn into flames of self-directed evolution...or human divinities. These men or women, while able through their initiations to proceed to other higher realms, choose to stay behind, to assist Mankind as a supreme guide or Instructor, living usually as a Nirmanakaya. The Nirmanakaya turns away from Nirvana and instead chooses to remain on earth for one purpose only....to serve Mankind in specific ways. When that service has been completed, the Nirmanakaya ends his time on planet Earth, and returns to Buddha State, to Nirvana.

It is in this state of Nirmanakaya that the Buddhas of Compassion...also known as the greatest of the Sages and Seers and super-holy men and women who passed through their times on this planet...strive through the ages of evolution to bring forth to Mankind the message, functions and powers of the divinity within the individual. It is the Nirmanakaya whose purpose is to be with certain sections of mankind in all ways, and by being with them, to continuously instil the powers of enlightenment in them by seeding the thoughts of self-sacrifice, self-forgetfulness, moral and spiritual beauty, mutual help and compassion...for them to become Buddhas of Compassion.....one of the noblest flowers of the human race, man-gods or human divinities.

Whether one can accept the concept of Buddha is, of course, completely up to the individual, but I for one have no doubt that the Buddha has existed and now exists as well.....I've seen and met enough people who are 'enlightened' and 'authentic' to satisfy myself of that existence in one form or another.

Irving Says

I'm sure that if you take just a little of your time right now you will quickly identify people you know, or know of, who fit the descriptions outlined above.

If you wish, make a list of them and show briefly what the main points are about their personality and life that appeals to you. Write down ALL their positive aspects in five columns. Such as; honest, reliable, sincere, caring, and so on. Have the same number of words in each column. Now, looking at their virtues, can you understand them? Are they clear to you? Have you seen them in others? Do you see them in you? How do you relate to their virtues and strengths? What do you need to do to improve those virtues in you?

Surprise yourself with how many of those virtues you already possess to different degrees. After all, if you can identify these positive qualities in others, then you must also posses them in yourself to some extent....otherwise how could you possibly 'know' them? So, maybe you're not the big, bad, prick you think you are? Wouldn't that be a shame!

For those interested in the life of Siddhartha Gautama, you may wish to obtain a copy of Sir Edwin Arnold's beautiful and inspiring poem about Gautama, called Light of Asia. Also, if you can find a copy of his magnificent book, Light of Asia, you will own something of rare value.

Chapter One - Brother Jon

I knew him and loved him for 75 years, longer than anyone else, except me.

Four weeks ago today as I write this, the Fat Lady sang her last song to Jon who died homeless, with no family close, in a little northern town in Oregon, near the Pacific Ocean. He had been single for twenty some years and had travelled to many places to find his Shangrila. Each time he settled we heard the same story: 'This is it, this place is fantastic. Golf courses are the best I've ever seen. And the women, perfect. They've got an outstanding junior hockey team and they serve Canadian beer. They have two churches in town that hold regular dances and will also provide me with a great spot to live, 'cause that's what they do for anyone who asks.' He loved to golf and dance. Sometimes he did both things at the same time....a crazy kid, that bro!

Two months later, or so, he would leave this 'wondrous' spot, (or was it 'wanderous' in his case?), looking for something better; before long we'd receive a call from him saying the same phrases as always 'this is it, etc'

During his working life Jon held many prestigious jobs; china and silver sales, credit card memberships and a variety of publishing responsibilities in large and small markets such as Phoenix, Houston, LA, etc., then north along the west coast and finally to Oregon.

When he left his marriage his only daughter (he also had a stepdaughter) disowned him completely because, he said, that she maintained he sexually abused her, which he consistently and vehemently denied. But he felt the separation intensely. Sometimes the pain overwhelmed him. Strangely, when he died, his daughter told us that she had followed him by Google and the computer for years...go figure!

Like most of us I guess, Jon had a few idiosyncrasies of the conscious and subconscious minds. I say 'guess' because I haven't meant 'most of us' yet. His behaviour was often seen as strange, in that there was an obvious hesitation that showed itself when he talked to you. My parents used to ask me about this as they couldn't understand what was happening....did I think he was 'slow'? I had a pat answer that I used with them, and all other people who asked me similar questions about Jon: That it was my fault.

On a dreary winter's Sunday morning, when he was seven and I was thirteen, we were at home alone as the folks were off to church. As often happened we began to play a little bit of 'rough house' and as one thing led to another we wound up in the folks bedroom, wrestling on Mom's bed which was the bed nearest the outside wall. On the floor, attached to the wall, was a regular kind of room oil heater or radiator....the old metal kind that looked like fifteen, two to three foot high fingers joined together.

The Buddha's Nose

This got a little hectic, as they often did with brothers, and in the heat of the 'battle' I flipped him off the bed and smack on to the radiator. He hit the back of his head with a dull thud, right on top of two of the fingers of the heater. It sounded like a ripe watermelon being dropped from a third floor window.

He was stunned, and now in retrospect I'm not sure whether he was fully conscious or not, because I became completely engrossed with what I had done, and the amount of blood that was flowing everywhere. I cried. Jon cried. That's not exactly right: we both *yelled and screamed AND cried!*

I had the presence of mind to phone our Uncle Jack (yes, we had a phone, not two cans and a long string). He was one of the many doctors in our family, and we loved him completely. He was a kind, quiet, sweet, generous man and I felt especially close to him. I mean it was he who taught me how a virgin birth could happen, when I was struggling with the myth of Jesus, and many other equally important questions were answered too. Like, boiler makers of a shot glass full of Rye Whiskey and a schooner of beer mixed in the same glass, (including the shot glass itself) were not especially good for the mind or body. How could I have been anything *but* close? And I don't know how many times he had stitched me up by then, but it was a lot. But for all the years I played hockey after that, Jack's stitching prowess grew and grew as I became his best customer, or so he said. I played goal for most of my career and that was in the days BEFORE masks or any other type of head protection. In my last year Jack told me he counted 65 stitches in my face alone during the season...that did it. Anyway, after the phone call he came right over with his bag of tricks and by the time the folks got home Jon was stitched and looking reasonably alright, given the circumstances. I got away with it! ***Almost.***

From that day to this I believe that experience was what caused Jon his slowness and spaciness...I was responsible. I've told him that, our parents and almost everyone else on the planet who has been interested in the story, but they've all tried to talk me out of it, with the most honourable of intentions: Hasn't worked! But finally I have learned to say something like 'ok, thanks I feel better now.' I don't think they believe me but it usually ends the discussion. Of course, I will believe I was responsible till the end of my duration...and maybe a couple of lives after that.

Fair well Jon, sweet pleasant memories go gently with you bro

Irving Says

Sometimes things happen in our lives which, try as we might to release their hold on us, will stay with us and affect our behaviour and the way we live. Some try writing themselves a letter and burn it, use a good therapist, try yoga, become hypnotised, smoke good dope, booze it up, change wives/husbands/partners, change jobs, sell their kids to the highest bidder, or whatever. But nothing seems permanent.

The Buddha's Nose

So here's what you do: HARDEN THE FUCK UP!! That's a phrase you hear all the time in Australia's Northern Territory and it fits almost all situations in life, when you think about it. It is great advice and I suggest you use it whenever you can. Come to terms with this and realize that this is a part of you and always will be. And the next time this arises, treat it like an old friend: give it time, space and love.

I'm talking about an engram, or special area of the brain, where the subconscious has been entirely subjugated to the condition itself. There are lots more engrams to discuss.

But, whenever possible, do what you can to resolve issues around the family, especially the kids, because they will probably be in your life longer than other people.

Sometimes, with kids and grown-ups too, there will be no solution....and that *IS* the solution.

Chapter Two - Farmer Steele and George

This story is absolutely true, at least to the extent that is possible, the tyrannies of time and distance being what they are.

When I was very young I was a sickly child, almost from when I came onto this planet on February twenty first, 1932. I was a mistake, not only not planned but also started out as a bastard...and now I'm a orphan, ain't life a kick in the head? The 'mistake' was some time later resolved when Mom and Dad married when she was about four months pregnant.

It was a Romeo and Juliet love encompassing even the traditional ladder up to the second storey window and whisking off in the dead of night. That was the beginning of a family dysfunction that became overwhelming for almost all of the players, but that whole story is for another time and place. By the way, even though it's there, there's no 'fun' in dys**fun**ction.

Bronchitis, pneumonia, allergies, asthma, poison ivy, colds and physical weakness was the package I began this journey with.

By the time I was twelve I had had pneumonia three times, the first two before penicillin had hit the market, so in both instances I saw the light at the end

15

of the tunnel and no one expected me to make my next birthday, or next breakfast, for that matter. But by the time I had my third dose the drug saved me and turned me towards ultimately meeting Farmer Steele.

At age thirteen I had become a complete rebel against authority. I see now why. My maternal grandfather was a very successful doctor in Toronto, as well as chairman of the Board of Education and team doctor to the Toronto Argonauts gridiron football team. He was a big man of big tastes and habits, filled with hubris and streaked with meanness....a frightful combination. I know because he was my doctor almost exclusively from my earliest days to about age twelve. My parents sent me to his cottage most summers for as long as I can remember and it was there that I was completely and totally under his control in all aspects of my life. He was one miserable, frightening bastard. He was the ultimate Authority Figure (AF) whenever any of us were in his presence, in whatever form that took either by phone, letter or in person. He was six feet three inches and over 300 pounds of immediate threat and plain fear! I see now that he was my main protagonist in my formative years. He just scared the bejeezus out of me.

My rebellion was against him, my parents, my coaches and my teachers. And it was intense! I caused as much trouble as possible in as many ways as possible. My reaction against authority was complete by the time I entered my teens and I still carry a hunk of it with me today.

The Buddha's Nose

One Saturday morning when I was fourteen, my Dad proudly came home early from work with a brand new company car. Beautiful...it was a Chevrolet coupe with hydromatic drive and a rumble seat. Right from the dealer's showroom, my friend. Got the picture? NEW!

What happened next was to change our family dynamics for ever. Dad had to get back to work and it was at that point that he made a decision that was to affect the lives of our entire family....he chose to leave the car home and take the bus back to the office. And Mom went out to do her usual Saturday shopping and visiting of old people and friends. The car and I were alone! And so were the keys.

I called three of my friends and told them I was coming over to pick them up in a few minutes and to be ready. I did and they were.

Once I had my cargo on board I became wild, I drove through the local park in two different directions, buzzed girl friends houses and then stomped on it. Two blocks from our house I tried to make a curve in the road but there was some sand down and as we began to slide I hit the brakes...............

Can you imagine the scene when the folks got home: police in the house, two ambulances parked, Uncle Jack stitching, neighbours standing on the front lawn, murmuring..... and no car.

The accident completely totalled two cars, injured everyone in our car but the other one, a twelve-cylinder Packard sedan was empty and parked at the time. I re-parked it up a neighbour's steep front yard hill. The brand new Chevy was gone and Dad was left having to explain to the police and his employer in New York just what the hell had happened and why.

That day I was lucky to be alive twice: one when we hit the Packard and two when Dad got home.

It was years later, when Dad and I were able to discuss it, but the pain and embarrassment I had caused him was never to leave me...and still hasn't, even though he left this world in 1986. I apologised more than once, and he always accepted it with class.

The car crash did it. Two days later Dad had made an appointment for me to meet with the Big Brother Movement. He drove me there, waited while I was indoctrinated, and gave me bus fare to get home.

I hated the authority figures at the BB. To me they were pansies and insincere, and I gave them nothing of myself. I didn't even understand why I was there so I made their life as miserable as possible.

Two weeks later after a few more unsuccessful visits they advised my parents that I was "incorrigible" and they could do nothing with me. That's right... *incorrigible!* As far as I was concerned that was all nothing but pure bullshit but I kept that thought to myself as I knew what happens when you pour gasoline on a fire.

I was in serious trouble and I knew it. All throughout this whole car experience Dad never hit me nor do I recall him even raising his voice. This was most unusual as in the past I had been the recipient of his ire on more than one occasion. Once when I had defied him and stayed too late at a dance and seeing he was waiting up for me, I then tried to climb up the outside of the two storey house in the middle of a raging winter, through my open bedroom window and into bed, without him knowing. When he found me in bed, he broke an oak bunk bed ladder over my head and knocked me colder than the proverbial. And the other time was when he told me three times to get off the phone and I didn't, so he yanked the receiver from me and cracked me across the face, broke my nose and bruised my face for weeks. I chuckle today at the great international debate on whether or not we should hit our kids when they're bad.

Chuck Poole was one of Dad's close friends. They had played hockey and baseball together and often boxed each other in the 'good old days.' In later years they had both wound up very successfully in the insurance business and remained in touch. Chuck had two sons, one was a model citizen and the other an acknowledged shit disturber. The 'disturber's' Dad had found a way to handle the boy... he sent him to work on a farm from which he presumably came back a healthy, well-disciplined, well adjusted young man.

"Eddie," Chuck said to Dad one day, "You're going to have to break this kid of yours before he runs right off the tracks and here's what you do.... send him to a working farm for the summer. There are lots of farmers looking for cheap help these days, just find a spot and kick the kid's ass down there."

The Buddha's Nose

Dad thought that was really good advice and in the paper next day was a farmer near Brantford Ontario looking for a young man to help out. He would pay room and board and a few bucks each week. Dad picked up the phone and made the deal right then and there.

When he told me about it I didn't want any part of it. I have worked on all three of my grandfather's farms and all I could see was his meaner-than-cat-shit-face staring at me. I rebelled!

The rebellion didn't last long. Dad made it clear in no uncertain terms that if I didn't take the deal he would have me arrested for stealing his company car. And he was serious. I agreed to go that same day.

The next day Farmer Steele met me at the Brantford station and so began a slice of my life that was to have serious long-term implications and complications that have stayed with me up until I write this now.

As we drove to the farm he told me what he expected of me. He owned two farms about a mile apart and I would be doing work at both of them. We would wake at 4am and the daily chores would be handled and then off to the daily workload. The family consisted of husband and wife and four daughters. He expected me to do what I was told, when I was told, and to not cause any trouble. He was a tall, wiry man in his middle to late forties with a soft voice and hard hands. He reminded me of a successful cowboy...like the guy from High Noon. He was definitely not someone to fool with.

The Buddha's Nose

I ate with the family that night, great food and lots of it. And around the table, loaded with more than enough of everything, sat Annie, the youngest daughter. Gorgeous......she reminded me of Elizabeth Taylor, with one leg shrivelled from polio. I was taken with her immediately and it helped that she was only about a year older than me. Can you sense the downfall happening??

Within a couple of days I was joining the kids in their daily dip in one of the two swimming holes on the property. The only rules were: never swim alone and always swim bare-bum.

By the end of the first week or so Annie and I had become closer as we found time to talk and enjoy each other's company. Then one day Farmer and Mrs Steele announced they were going in to town to shop and that they'd be some time. The three girls were all working off the premises and that left just Annie and me and our respective libidos.

Believe it or not, up in the hay loft is where we found ourselves, doing what young kids did as they tested their senses and sexuality. There really was such a thing as "a roll (or was it a 'role?') in the hay."

We were both novices at the art of sex and fear and trepidation had slowed down the process to almost a halt when we heard the most frightening sound of all...... Farmer Steele's voice calling out for us. They had come home much, much sooner than expected.

Oh shit!! He was coming closer to the barn...and then the door downstairs opened and he was in the building. We were frozen stiff, unable to think or act

...not even able to look at each other. Now he was moving around below us and then he was at the foot of the ladder.

"I know you're up there, come down now."

.............the original pregnant pause

"Now, or I'm coming up"

We couldn't speak. I thought I would faint.

Then we heard him climbing the steps and my life passed before me: I was sorry, for everything, to everyone, no exceptions, for ever and ever, amen.

We were frozen in time and space...couldn't move, couldn't talk.

And then he was standing in front of us as we cringed in the hay. He held a pitch fork in his hand and his face was crimson. I remember it well; the scene, the smell of fear and the pounding of my heart in my throat...strange place for a heart.

"Both of you, come down now." We did, somehow.

"Annie, go to the house and stay there in your room until I come for you."

"And you, get all your things packed and get in the truck, NOW!"

We drove for about 45 minutes without a sound being uttered. Hanging on the back wall of the truck were two rifles, a shot gun and a 22 Winchester. A Smith and Wesson six shooter was holstered on the driver's side door, and I knew they were all loaded, and I wondered.....

He pulled us up close to the train platform with the instruction to sit still. He left to get the ticket and I considered breaking for it. But where would I go? And what would I do for money? And what if he found me, would my 'wondering' become a reality?

He came back to the truck and leaned through the window with the instructions, "Get out, get your bag from the back and follow me."

He walked briskly, with me in tow, to one of the waiting carriages. Stopped there at the steps and turned to me.

"Get up those steps, you rotten little bastard and be thankful that I didn't kill you. Now get out of my sight. *You'll never amount to anything, you lousy little shit.*"

I scurried. And for what seemed to be an interminable wait the train finally chugged away from Farmer Steele. Or so I thought....because, you see, he's still here as big and scary as ever.

Introducing George

For me an engram is a self-made section of the deepest aspect of the brain where there resides the result of an extreme experience usually manifested through the direction, either direct or not, of an Authority Figure whose impact over you is so strong that your subconscious cannot or does not refrain from accepting his or her message and turning it into a form of habit that is so deeply implanted that we don't know that it is a habit. These engrams form a large and intricate place in the subconscious mind. This subconscious mind is what I call GEORGE.

George is comprised of engrams, habits, behaviours, neuroplasticity, cellular memories, unconscious behaviours such as breathing and blinking, heredity, environment, atavistic tendencies and spirituality. George is responsible for well over eighty percent of my behaviour. I am programmed by him in just about all matters good or bad, positive or negative, right or wrong. He drives me daily from one of life's scenarios to the next.

Through the use of the implanted engram concept George is able to direct me. He is neither bad nor good. He just is! He's like a young child, acting on what he is told without the ability to think through those actions clearly.

Subconscious tendencies are many and varied, depending on the predominant engram or engrams in place at the time, and the circumstances in front of me right then and there.

For more information on engrams turn to Chapter Three for the Full Monty.

"You'll never amount to anything."

George can be a little trouble-maker, but I can teach him to alter his habits if they don't fit my requirements and wishes. You do that through *your conscious mind*. But first, his major negative or hurtful behaviours must be identified and ultimately resolved.

Authority Figures (AFs) are people, places, things, music, art, food, cars, money, clothes, houses and so on that step in front of George at some point and state un-categorically that: THIS IS WHAT YOU *WILL* BELIEVE....NOW! But for the sake of this discourse I am limiting myself exclusively to the AFs of the human type.

By the time I was nineteen I had already served three years in the insurance business, first with my dad's company as the world's worst office boy and filing clerk, then with one of the world's leading Brokers and then with a large American company situated in Toronto, covering the entire country. Before my 20th birthday I had a company car, expense account and was travelling regularly as a Special Agent, an impressive term for a company rep. But even as far back as then I had a strong interest in my behaviours and those around me. I had already figured out that, '*I could meet my attitude coming around the corner.*'

It was easy.....insurance was a breeze for me, maybe because my Dad and his Dad had both been senior executives and the cellular structure had been passed on to me. Whatever the reason, the company offered me a huge promotion, which I asked for time to consider. I did and one week later I went to my boss and resigned. He was shocked and asked me for an explanation. I couldn't give anything that made sense!

Two more jobs followed and in each case similar circumstance occurred.... as soon as I had been approached for extra responsibility I left and got an even better job almost immediately. This process went on in Canada and then later in the USA when I and my young family moved to California to "increase my knowledge of the business."

"You'll never amount to anything"

Later, I returned to Toronto and had been home just a short time when my Dad told me that he had run into a friend of his who was President of a large Life Insurance Company and was looking for someone with my background. He asked Dad to ask me to phone him. I did, we met for lunch the next day and I was hired on the spot as an executive forming a brand new division of the company. Eighteen months later the President was advised that the board would like to appoint him to the Chair and asked that he look for his replacement. One day at the club he told this to my Dad and added that he felt the job would be mine in the near future.

Dad told me of the conversation that night and a month later I resigned with the excuse that my wife was homesick and it shocked everyone involved. At a going away party held at the top hotel in the city, my boss pulled me aside and said that he understood my dilemma having to deal with an unhappy wife but he was amazed that I could throw away this 'golden opportunity' and he confessed that he couldn't understand how I could do that but wished me well.

Years later he and his wife visited us in our nice apartment on the harbour at Darling Point, Sydney, and still referred to what had happened back then. It still didn't make sense to him, particularly seeing that I had a new wife from the one he knew. I honestly didn't know what to tell him..... because I didn't know myself!

The Buddha's Nose

Throughout my career the pattern maintained itself....in Toronto, in Los Angeles, in Hong Kong, in London and in Sydney......obtain a great job, find it easy to be effective, increase my power in my field, impress my boss with my results and client relationships, be offered a higher position based on my own results, take the offer under advisement......and resign. And start the process all over again somewhere else.

As the years went by I became more and more involved in psychology, the study of which intrigued me, and before long I found myself completely engrossed in human behaviours ....others and mine. *Especially mine!*

"You'll never amount to anything"

Over the years I received a number of certificates, diplomas and degrees and the deeper I got into my studies of the psyche, the more I became convinced that I was a slave to the past, a coward to the so-called present (which is really just the immediate NOW, otherwise it's just the past or the future), and blinded to the future. I knew this had to change and I was going to have to face the reality of my own experiences and deal with those that I could identify as negative, hurtful and unproductive.

But how? What was holding me back? Where did the responsibility lie for my mistakes, my missed opportunities. Why had I hurt people? Why had I betrayed them? Why had I done the wrong thing, when

I knew it was wrong at the time? Why had I been such a louse as often as I had?

"You'll never amount to anything"

Slowly the answers came. The gigantic impact of engrams in my life started to surface through my conscious mind and pointed an accusatory finger directly at George and the impetus of his form of hypnosis over me. *I was hooked and I saw it!!*

Congratulations Farmer Steele and George, you seemed to have manipulated my life's direction like a drunken puppeteer pulling frayed strings, and I'm very glad to be here, and now maybe I can help others see their own light...their Buddha's Nose.

Irving Says

As a father there is a paramount responsibility that is yours as soon as the sperm hits the egg, it begins then and lasts till the kid is out of the house fending for him/her self. Kick them out when they reach 18 at the oldest. Or, if they just won't go, YOU go....grab your wife and get the hell out of there as fast as you can. If you have to, buy a tent, live in a dumpster, find a comfortable cave at the beach....anything. Just go! Retrospect would teach you that it is the best thing that ever happened to you since you first heard those three ancient, frightening, happy, exciting, motivating words, "Honey, I'm pregnant."

A daughter's mother should take the lead when sex talks become the issue of the day. You, as the dad, should play a secondary role and provide solid backup support to your wife. Mothers have a way about them, they have a tendency to talk to their daughters in some kind of primeval code that you and I as brothers will never, ever understand or decipher.....don't even bother trying! Leave well enough alone.

If you are a single father, find an appropriate woman to help. I can't give you any better advice because I haven't had a reason to bring up a daughter without the support of a woman, or my parents, beside me, so, I have no bloody idea!

As a son's father you carry with you some serious responsibilities, as well as a genetic makeup that includes 50% of your son's very being. Here's one thing you don't do about sex talk with your son: don't do what my dad, Fast Eddie, did when I was fifteen.

I had three buddies over at the house one Sunday morning, while the folks were at church. We were doing our usual thing of finding ways and means to create trouble somewhere, somehow...and doing quite well at it, I might add, when the folks arrived home sooner than expected (usually Mom dallied to have discussion with the minister in charge).

"OK boys, into the car, we're going to the movies," instructed dad.

"The movies?" I said. "On a Sunday in Toronto? I don't think so." It was only 1947.

"Yes, movies," said the Fast One.

When we arrived downtown, sure enough something was certainly happening at one of the theatres, there was a line half way up the block of what appeared to be mostly males, and on the marquee it said "Sins of the Fathers."

In we went, the place was packed, the coloured movie, on a big screen (a real novelty back then), began and before long Eddie Johnston our friend and probably two dozen other guys in the room were puking their guts out. I was so dizzy that I had to sit on the floor so I wouldn't keep falling off the chair. The movie was an army film about syphilis and just how bad it could be if you wound up with the wrong woman who was 'diseased.' Shit house mouse, it was fierce!

We were all deep purple (I often wondered in later years if that was originally where the song Deep Purple came from...had some musician seen Sins of the Fathers too?) The drive home was in total silence and when we got there Fast Eddie directed us into our living room, where he held court.

"Now listen you guys, now that you've seen the movie you understand that sex can be nice or not so nice. And because you are all now dating girls, I need to tell you something that the movie didn't tell you."

Believe me, we were all still shaking from the experience on film, so we sat still and listened.

"Any girl can be made, providing it's the right guy, the right time and the right place. Don't ever forget that."

Obviously I never have.

That was the extent of my dad's discussion with me about sex. There was never another word about it from then on. As far as I can recall, my buddies and I never discussed it again either. No wonder I still have an unconscious fear of sex!

Life since those days has changed dramatically; computers, mobile telephones, ipods, ipads, trips to the moon and now Mars, cars that park themselves and on and on it goes. But what hasn't changed is parental responsibility towards children's sexual enlightenment. The ancients called it Dharma; duty, responsibility and obligation. Dharma fits today as much as it did then, maybe even more.

Chapter Three – All About Engrams

Everything you would ever want to know about engrams if you ever wanted to know about them in the first place

ENGRAM: A neuronal pathway of the brain becomes activated by a particular sensory series of repetitions on the one issue, until the response becomes stabilised and automatic. This occurs after a familiar stimulus from outside the brain, registers itself on the brain...which automatically leads to the implementation of the appropriate Engram.

You can see from the Farmer Steele story just how devastating Authority Figures can be to our life-long behaviour, through the creation of their imposed negative engrams upon you and George. People such as our parents, family members, clergy, school teachers, music teachers, politicians, cops, firemen, bosses, ...even theatre ushers, garbage collectors, gym instructors, husbands or wives, or anyone who we consider a 'force,' can manipulate George, to the extent that he will react the same way ALWAYS, until you change his behaviour. To do that you must see and understand what needs to be changed....and CHANGE IT.

This engram is deeply-learned and consists of electrical impulses in the brain that have been concretised through neurons releasing hundreds of chemical receptor molecules that create electrical activators that alter the brain patterns automatically.

The chemical changes that have been established, by directly changing the brain patterns are the result of change in behaviour.

Therefore: **to change our behaviour, we must change our brain patterns by changing our brain chemical balance.**

The Process of Stimulus - Response Change:

1. Look at the Brain **Stimulus;**

2. Then the **Response Patterns** that exist;

3. Then the **CREATION of NEW RESPONSE PATTERNS.**

A Stimulus-Response is also known as a "Cognitive Memory Pattern."

An Example of Positive Personal Engrams: "Young kids make me happy to hear and see them play."

An example of Negative Personal Engrams: "I rage at parents who hurt their kids."

The Buddha's Nose

It sometimes seems as though I have no choice about the stimulus-response mechanism that has been set in place over the years. It's possible that some or many of my engrams may be the result of certain personality traits being "obviously" or "accidentally" activated by random experiences I had many years or even many lives ago.

For example, I may be very punctual as a personality trait, and may respond to people who are perpetually late with anger, frustration, lack of confidence in them and a strong doubt about their other virtues. This Engram of mine may have been developed as:

1. The result of my father constantly harping on the need to be on time to be successful. "OBVIOUS " ACTIVATION

~or~

2. I may have arrived late for a very important job interview and lost the job because of it. "ACCIDENTAL" ACTIVATION

~or~

3. In my immediate past life I may have been a perpetual late arriver, who was filled with an insatiable need for recognition (a Soul/Personality Drive) and achieved it by bringing attention to myself (a form of DISPLAY). I may have been late "once too many" and been severely punished by my father ... and through that punishment my lesson was learned and I was no longer late.

In example 1, my Engram may well have been established through the "OUTSIDE" influence of my father's stern rule and the fear I had for him on a physical level.

~or~

In example 2, I may have learned my lesson for myself, without any outside influence, from the "INSIDE" result caused by my own experience.

~or~

In example 3, this Past Life condition may be the result of one of two possibilities:

1. In my immediate past life I may have been punished severely by my mother for a regular transgression that resulted in my being late until she could take it no longer.

2. I may have been witness to a severe punishment handed out to one of my friends, sister or brother, whose reaction to the punishment was so intense that it has left a Permanent Impression on me, so strong that it was as if the situation happened to me directly.

Some other Personality Traits that may have led to "OBVIOUS" or "ACCIDENTAL" Engrams:

Aggressiveness;

Shyness;

Neatness;

Extravagance;

Frugality; and

Tardiness.

If you wish, think of some more in your case...and decide whether they are obvious or accidental, and positive or negative

_____

_____

To review:

An ENGRAM is a Stimulus-Response Patterning Process that is a basic mechanism of the brain that incorporates Electrochemical patterns, Emotional feedback loops and Emotional states that are processed

An ENGRAM is a Stimulus-response that has become STABILISED by the development of a LEARNED PATTERN that operates without choice

An ENGRAM can be POSITIVE or NEGATIVE, depending upon how it was originally created by your brain, and how it now affects your life

An ENGRAM can be created through OBVIOUS procedures, or through ACCIDENTAL procedures.

The Buddha's Nose

To identify a POSITIVE ENGRAM from a NEGATIVE ENGRAM, use the following terms from NOW ON:

A POSITIVE ENGRAM is a PENGRAM

A NEGATIVE ENGRAM is a NENGRAM

The Stimulus part of a PENGRAM or a NENGRAM can be one or more of:

VISUAL;

AUDITORY;

KINESTHETIC;

OLFACTORY (sense of smell); and

GUSTATORY (sense of taste).

The Response part of a PENGRAM or a NENGRAM can be one or more of:

VISUAL;

AUDITORY;

KINESTHETIC;

OLFACTORY; and

GUSTATORY.

The learned or acquired response pattern does <u>not</u> have to involve the same senses as required for the related stimulus.

This is due to certain types of brain cells now identified in the cerebellum, in addition to the billions of nerve cells, or neurons that are activated through the "thought process" as well as hormonal secretion.

The number of possible inter-connections between these cells during the thought process "is greater than the number of atoms in the universe" (Ornstein & Thompson).

Therefore, the "brain-link" between a Stimulus (from the senses) and a Response (such as fear, pain or pleasure) are PERCEPTIONS that are LEARNED

Irving Says

What we can learn, we can un-learn!!

To do that, we need to create mind states. A mind state is a planned response of excellence, e.g.:

1. A time when your performance was exceptional for you;

2. A time when you surprised yourself with your own ability;

3. A situation in your life when you excelled beyond your expectation.

Think of ONE OF EACH:

The Buddha's Nose

1. _____

2. _____

3. _____

Each example requires the same criteria for the development of a Mind State, by beginning with:

Identification of ONE RESPONSE OF EXCELLENCE

Return to the scene (VISUALISE the picture as you remember it)

Add what you SAW when you were in the picture (DO NOT DISASSOCIATE OR SEE THE SCENE FROM A POINT OF VIEW WHERE YOU ARE OUTSIDE LOOKING IN);

Add what you HEARD;

Add what you FELT;

Add what you SMELT; and

Add what you TASTED.

To all of the above add the original sense of EXCITEMENT, SATISFACTION or CONFIDENCE that went with the original scene

Having accomplished all of the above, think of the first word that comes to your mind that accurately sums up ALL of the above sensations.......this will now be your CUE WORD

Finally, give this entire exercise a COLOUR that comes to your mind that most adequately describes the ENTIRE SCENE

Now the entire technique for creating a Mind State

1. Re-create the entire scene of EXCELLENCE, including ALL of the sensations that accompanied it originally.....see yourself BACK IN IT AGAIN, not as an interested observer, but as the PARTICIPANT;

2. Imagine a CIRCLE OF EXCELLENCE directly in front of you on the floor, and PAINT IT your COLOUR;

3. Let as much air out of your lungs as possible, and follow that with a DEEP BREATH......hold it and step into the Circle;

4. While you stand there, INTENSIFY the memory of that special scene or event as much as possible by Iintensive focus, called CATHEXIS; and

5. Enjoy the strong sense of CONFIDENCE and SELF IMAGE that naturally goes with the occasion.

Now, go through the above sequence of events again ... only this time add your CUE WORD after number two and before number 3.

Stay in the Circle this time as LONG AS THE EXPERIENCE REMAINS WITH YOU.

Go through the entire experience twice more before finishing the exercise.

Changing Patterns Of Nengrams (a negative engram)

Let's use JEALOUSY as a typical NENGRAM.

Jealousy usually comes from our personal lack of self-security or self image.

To change the STIMULUS, we need to change our feelings about ourselves in this situation.

This is accomplished by selecting THREE positive memories that people have left you with ABOUT YOURSELF, e.g., you have beautiful eyes, you have a beautiful smile, you have a lovely voice.

Give each of these memories COLOURS, FEELINGS and SOUNDS as well as any other SENSATIONS that were present at the time of the compliment.

Give each one a CUE WORD, e.g., "eyes," "smile," voice."

The Buddha's Nose

Try this experiment the next time you feel pangs of jealousy

Success Comes From Practice & Confidence

Engrams are a form of Self-Referencing, or Programming, that can be so strong we often cannot move past our Self-Developed limitations or boundaries. To do so would mean that we would be forced to accept the fact that we could, and might, be wrong. This would require our concretised Self-Perceptions to be incorrect.

Many of our Engrams are a direct result of our own genetic thought patterns, in other words what we've learned from our parents thinking (even when we were in the womb), from Authority Figures that have impacted our life, or from atavistic tendencies, including past lives.

Chapter Four - A Re-Visit With Farmer Steele

While I was with Farmer Steele there occurred an experience that changed my life and has remained with me, loud and clear.

On a hot August morning, Farmer Steele announced to me that he wanted to go up to the other farm they owned for a special job that needed doing immediately ... I was the one who had drawn the short straw it seemed, judging by the expressions on the other family members faces around the breakfast table that day; little did I know!

Before we left, four of the farm hands loaded a trailer to overflowing with a huge grey female horse that was apparently destined to handle really heavy jobs that happen from time to time around a farm. She was BIG, at least 147 vertical hands high. I may be exaggerating a bit here. Since I had been there I had only seen her in the paddock or at feeding time....I thought she was a free-loader, but boy was I wrong!

About a mile up the road we turned into a neatly laid out farm that was obviously intended for various types of planting items such as corn, tomatoes, wheat, hay, etc. We drove past the farm house and well on into the back paddocks until we came to what seemed to be acreage that had been levelled but had nothing growing on it yet.

We stopped there and the guys removed the big grey (I can't recall her name, but I wish I could). At one end of the field lay a strange looking contraption that I was soon to become personally involved with beyond my wildest dreams. It was rusty in colour, about eight feet wide and twelve feet long, flat framed and constructed of steel. The outside frame was held in place by a cross bar also steel spaced about two feet apart from front to back. Two cross bars were fixed from end to end about equal distance from each other. A 'V' shaped contraption was at the front where the horse would be harnessed.

Now for the best part! At equal distance of about two feet, covering the entire underside of the four inch frame were spike-like steel 'prodders' intended to break up the ground and create deep lines where planting could be started: larger at the top where they affixed to the frame and slowly reduced in size until they finally looked like some kind of ancient evil weapon of mass destruction. Got the picture? Good.

The angry sun beat down relentlessly and the horse flies, the size of B47s, were already forming a welcoming committee.

As the grey was being attached to the frame, Farmer Steele decided to let me in on what was going to happen next.

"I want you to take the lead in both hands and walk about three feet behind the frame as the horse pulls it along.

Your job is to keep the horse straight in the grooves that you can see marked. Finish one line, then turn the horse and go to the next one. Got it? Ok. ***Now, listen to me: do not under any conditions ride on this frame, it is very dangerous if you do. Always walk behind the frame. Do you understand?"***

I nodded knowingly.

They left after they saw me walk with the grey half way up the first line. The next time they would see me, Doctor Death would be knocking.

It was close to high noon when I finished the first half of the field. The heat was intense and the horse flies were holding board meetings to decide where and when they should attack us next..... legs, arms, shoulders, necks...where? At least the old grey had a tail, I wasn't quite that lucky.

It was then that I made the decision: I'm going to ride on this sucker now, but should I ride on the front near the horse, or on the back. Not the back, the front! Up I went, tucked the lead over my shoulder, except for the small amount I needed to direct the horse......Giddyup!!!

I may have been the world's first corn field surfer and certainly I was almost the last.

We were going along swimmingly well when big grey must have been bitten on one of her least protected areas, because she lurched suddenly, and before I knew what had happened I was on the ground, on my back, under the frame, unable to move an inch. To this day I don't know exactly how it happened and also to this day the picture is clear in my mind...the smells, the sounds, the flies, old grey, her swishing tail, the fear... I was shit scared!

Everything became quiet. If the horse moved two feet I would die. She stood sedately, swishing and stomping one of her back feet. I could see her from where I lay. The flies attacked us both... I saw them clearly as they went for her rump and under the tail region. She stomped at that, most of all it seemed. Well, wouldn't you?

It was somewhere around noon, the sun beat down and I knew I was going to die. I couldn't move anything except my head a bit. And then it happened!

She swished, stomped and even neighed with her gross discomfort and, suddenly, from out of nowhere a deep male voice of authority called out, "Whoa horse, whoa." She settled. That was the beginning of about an hour and a half of my personal hell. They told me later that I talked of a voice soothing the grey and me. So help me, she didn't move forward or backward in all that period of time... nothing.

By then the pains were taking over. The flies were having a field day, you'll pardon the pun, and I and the grey were both seriously suffering as each minute crept by.

One of the farm hands came to pick me up to take me back for lunch. He saw the predicament and released old grey immediately. But I was another story because he couldn't even budge the frame off me. He returned with two more hands and they were able to eventually move the frame enough to slowly release me from where I was wedged.

I don't know how many times I heard the voice say "whoa" that day but each time I hear that expression even now, in my dreams, all these years later, I still react. Sometimes the same strong voice still clearly calls out my name during the day or night, but I do nothing about it because I know it's my friend. I also know I'm not schitzo!... even though others might well debate that with me.

I should have known then that Farmer Steele and I were never going to be the best of buddies. He gave me a good going over that day, but I got off work so that Mrs Steele could nurse me and deal with my bites and the poison that comes from too many of them at one time. I liked her...and her daughters, I might add. I was alright the next morning though and things were back to normal.

Later, through my studies I found out what that voice was. It was my Psychopomp, a term used in the esoteric world to describe a portion of the human soul. Once I learned that I never again doubted whether or not I had a soul. I knew it had talked to me out on the steaming hot field that day. That voice will always be with me. From time to time even today my Psychopomp still calls out my name, just to let me know he's still there, I think. In later years it was the primary reason for me studying Esoteric Psychology with Dr Douglas Baker.

Irving Says

If you think there's something more to life than *nothing* then do yourself a favour and check things out. The true Path of Enlightenment is fraught with potholes, lies, hubris, bullshit and disappointments. But that doesn't mean that it isn't a path that you can take carefully, cautiously and at your own pace. It has many side roads that will present themselves to you as you search for meaning, reality and hope. That's all there too.

By studying the path of ancient wisdom or metaphysics you can feel very comfortable with what you learn because you can accept or reject all or any part of it and that should make you feel as though you are in control. You don't have to be swayed by other people's opinions or directions. You won't be forced to agree to anything or swear allegiance to anything or anybody. It isn't necessary to accept strange, impractical myths. You can be you, think your own thoughts, be as opinionated as you wish, be frightened at the mysteries of life, and feel hope growing in the sensation of knowing there is something out there much greater than you, much larger above you than you are above the animals of the planet. The quest is to look for and find it.

As a human being, we have the right and privilege to look for answers, find them and live them, any time we care to put in the hard yards. Anything worthwhile has been earned, nothing worthwhile comes without a cost, that's my experience.

The first thing of real value that you may well find out is that you have a soul.... and a personality that often tries to kick the crap out of it. The soul can show itself to you in more than one way, but certainly the most pronounced for me was that day on Farmer Steele's field, when I lay under the contraption that had me pinned and a huge grey horse, bitten painfully time after time by horse flies, refused to move other than to swish her tail, because a male voice coming from nowhere told her time after time after time not to.

No doubt many of us have had similar experiences in our lives but haven't bothered to put two and two together. Maybe that's because a long time ago you decided that there sure as hell is nothing special about you....and maybe you are still harbouring under that same illusion, but it ain't true!.......we're ALL special in some form or other.

So, get up off the couch and go huntin'. The prey is YOU!

Chapter Five - Douglas Baker

In the spring of 1970, my wife at the time and I moved our family back to Toronto from Los Angeles. We drove a recently purchased Ford Woodie station wagon and pulled behind a brand new 25 foot house trailer. The trip incorporated many unintentional consequences: one was a meeting of the Canadian Mounties who had tracked me from California where they had thought I had been part of a criminal activity. Later I was cleared, but having three Mounties knock at my door was pretty scary. That was one group of Authority Figures who came and went peacefully in my life. I never rebelled against their power.

A few months later we had purchased a lovely home in Toronto and I had settled into a new and challenging executive job, when one bleary winter's night we went into town to hear a man named Dr Douglas Baker speak on metaphysics. Light snow flakes were swirling holus bolus in the icy wind streams when we entered the basement meeting room of a local Christian church. Little did I suspect that this was to be the beginning of a whole new aspect of my life.

By the end of the first break I was more than ready to get out of the joint... Douglas was filling the room with more hubris than I could handle. But, when I went to get my car from the church parking lot, a snow storm had hit and we were completely snowed in. I went back to hear more as I saw no other choice.

By the time the session was over I was a fan of Douglas'. I talked to him briefly afterwards and he was kind and considerate to me. I gave him my home address for some reason, I don't recall why right now.

The next morning, a Saturday, the door bell rang at about 10 am. There was Douglas, bright eyed and bushy-tailed. Being very Pommy, we naturally offered him a cup of tea and things began. From that day on, until his death three years ago, I was first his student, and then he became my mentor and friend for over 40 years.

He had a proposition for us: loan him $500, needed to publish what he said would be his first of many books, and he would have the money back to us within six weeks. For some unknown reason I agreed. In 1970 five hundred bucks was a lot of money, not that it isn't today, but I felt it was a sure thing that we'd get the money back. Well, we had it back in just *four* weeks....no interest included, but I was soon to learn that that was Douglas.

Douglas was a single man all his life. He was married to humanity's dilemmas and his own frailties. During WWII he had been injured more than once and carried shrapnel pieces around in his body till the end. Also, he had been struck by lightning three times.... a record I think. And not many people who had been hit that often have lived to tell the tale.

The Buddha's Nose

He began appearing before the public by teaching school in the roughest section of London, then moved into the medical field receiving his degrees as a physician and surgeon, both at an advanced age of over 40. And then he launched into the field of Esoteric Psychology or Metaphysics, primarily through his international Claregate College, which, I'm proud to say, I had a part to play in its formation in 1972.

During his life he gave more than 15,000 live lectures on the subject of Ancient Wisdom, 127 eBooks are already published and available in over 200 countries, has produced hundreds of DVDs, MP3lectures, News Letters, Correspondence Courses as well as commercial films. And in his spare time he had to put up with donkeys like me.

Many years later Douglas, from time to time, would present seminars in our complementary medicine college, Gracegrove, in Newcastle, New South Wales.

He was never on Easy Street, or anywhere close to it. Money was always tight. His travel expenses around the world bit deeply into his income from Claregate and, as frugal as he was, it was always going to be difficult to make ends meet. They never really did, if you know what I'm saying.

One day he was providing a series of lectures at Gracegrove, our College in Newcastle, NSW and after an afternoon session on reincarnation, he returned to his hotel for a rest. An hour later he called me at my office at the college to come over for a talk, which I did, the affect of which is still with me today.

When I arrived at his room, it was in semi-darkness and he was obviously somewhere between asleep and awake, but in a moment he was on full sharp mode. He told me how impressed he was with what we were doing with the college, the subjects we were teaching, the student base we had built and the plans we were implementing for the future. I thanked him, and then he dropped it on me: because I was one of his 'ten inner sanctum' people, meaning those very close to him and his work, he wanted me to have a special gift of thanks for what I had done for him. He gave me the name of one of my most important past lives, a Bishop in England in the 1500s, and suggested that I research this info in detail. I did and was amazed.

Leaving the room that afternoon I still recall how strange I felt. I was cockeyed, staggering from one side of the hall, as I went for the elevator, to the other. I was bouncing from wall to wall. When I reached the elevator Joe Hayes, Douglas' long time assistant, saw my plight and when I told him what had happened in the room he took charge of me and brought me back to reality. He knew what to do because he had been there himself.

Not long afterwards one of our students' mother died suddenly and the family came to me with the request that I perform the eulogy. I resisted and they persisted: they won.

I couldn't believe how easy it was to do what I did that day. It was as if I was wearing a purple robe, red sandals and an ancient silver incense burner around my neck. Well, I may be stretching it a bit here, but you get the idea don't you? It was life-changing for me.

Irving Says

If you wish, name the people in your life that have had the most dramatic affect on you.

Of all the teachers you have had, who was the best, and why?

Who was the worst teacher you ever had, and why?

What single teacher did you learn the most from, and exactly what was it?

And then, give thanks.

Chapter Six - Fast Eddie

In my family we had many nicknames for each other that we used depending on the circumstances. Usually Jon called me 'bear' and I called him 'bro.'

When Jon and I became aware that we were taller than Mom we began calling her 'Short,' which she did not like at all. So, we called her that as often as possible, but NOT before a full baked dinner, for fear of some foreseeable consequences that would not be to our advantage.... after dinner, ok.

Fast Eddie was the name Jon and I gave our Dad, and it stuck right to the end. All Dad's friends called him "Eddie." Not Mom, she called him 'Ed,' or, when the shit really hit the fan, it was "EDWIN."

It was strange though that Dad had only one nickname for Jon: that was 'Jonny.' But for me, a slew: I wonder now why I earned them and Jon apparently didn't... I'm just saying.

Speed, speedy, speeder, mugs, mugsy and shit-bird all applied to me. I'm only kidding about shit-bird, that's what Mom called me at times. I certainly got the oft-repeated 'bastard,' 'little bastard,' 'horse's ass' and 'sonofabitch'... but they were, more or less, terms of endearment... yeah, right!

Fast Eddie taught me to skate, play hockey, baseball,

box... and shoot pool. The pool thing didn't turn out so well as in later years I was often caught playing snooker when I was supposed to be in school.... I hated school! As well, he had the patience to teach me to drive. It was always an experience for me to go with Dad to a hockey game, baseball game or a fight because it seemed like most of the people in the auditorium, rink or park knew Eddie Heaton. I felt like a celebrity being accompanied by my own personal body guard.

Up until the time my folks met, Dad had been a 'roust-about-town' who worked at professional sports, earned his money playing hockey in the winter, baseball in the summer and boxing year round, and Mom was a debutante of some kind. Things changed extremely quickly when the two found out there was a pregnancy now to contend with. Although I was in the 'oven' then I suspect that I could probably feel the extreme distaste that Mom's dad, JW felt for me. In later years he had many an opportunity to show me just what the hell he thought of me each time my parents sent me to his farms and cottages for the summer months. Alone, without them, I was fair fodder for his hate for Dad.

As far back as my simple little mind can go, Dad was travelling. As an insurance executive of a major national company he had to visit branches, agents and brokers regularly around the country as well as deal with his staff, to say nothing of handling the almost regular traumas created at home by his oldest boy, namely me. Jon was a pussycat in comparison.

The Buddha's Nose

Fast Eddie was a good man who suffered fools very badly. Outside of his family he took no prisoners. If he saw someone hurting someone else he would immediately interfere and do whatever it took. He had a vicious left hook and right cross and no fear in using them when the situation called for it.... at the ball park or the subway, or wherever. He was not a big guy, but I always felt completely safe around him.... except when he lost his temper with **me.** Yoiks!

The last time I saw Dad was in 1985 when Jon and I made arrangements for him to move into a very nice old age home in Toronto. His major complaint was that the place was filled with "old bastards." We had lunch with him that day and after the meal we talked together about this and that until finally he began to cry. It surprised the bejesus out of us because we'd never seen him do that before. Even when the three of us buried Mom a few years prior we saw no sign of grief in his countenance.

As we left the home we cuddled each other and there were still tears in Fast Eddie's eyes, but we straightened up, said goodbye, told him we loved him and left, as he turned away...... big boys don't cry: bullshit!

We were walking to the car when we passed the steps of a friendly looking church and decided to plunk down on their inviting steps to get our emotions under control. Bad choice! We both began to cry and before long neither of us could stop. People were walking by and, seeing our state were offering their assistance, which we thankfully declined. When Bro and I talked about the experience in later years we were not at all sure how long we sat there but it was at least thirty minutes, maybe substantially longer.

Fast Eddie possessed certain moral philosophies that I respected very much, for example; love a dog and you'll always know where you stand. It was important for him to look after the homeless every year at Christmas, not because he was a religious man, he wasn't, but he felt their pain. During the year he gave to a number of charities. Dad felt, and said so more than once, that just because my wife (read wives) and I had divorced, she (they) were always part of his family and his mood and thinking on that subject never changed. He believed that children were meant to look after their parents as old age took over and inactivity and sickness became their burdens: I saw him do that with both his parents for years, and struggle financially while he did it. He was a stickler for truth: ask him a question at your risk because he'd always come back with his truth, so be ready. He applied that rule in all aspects of his life. There were many others, some of which were just plain good manners, such as, always give a standing lady a seat on the bus first because she's a lady and second because she may be pregnant, never butt in where you're not wanted, always treat women with the respect they deserve, and don't marry someone just because they're a great fuck.

Fast Eddie wasn't perfect by a long shot, but he was the best Dad *I* ever had!.... at least in this life.

The Buddha's Nose

Irving Says

If you wish, think about your own father. What specifically could you have done to improve your relationship with your Dad?

Of all the things he has left you with, what is the most important?

What do you think was the major mistake he made in his life?

Right now, when you are thinking of him, write down exactly what you see.

Now, what do you feel?

What could he have done better for you?

What could you have done better for him?

Chapter Seven - My Grandad's Knee
I Never Sat There

John Wesley Russell, M.D., my maternal grandfather was an obnoxious, miserable, offensive, arrogant, powerful giant of a man who bullied people and made them feel inferior... a real horse's ass. And yet here's the rub, he was also a life-saver. I know because he saved mine at least twice... maybe more!

He was about six feet two inches tall, weighed 300 to 350 pounds, was quick on his feet, slow on his patience and strong on his self-righteousness.

He had one of the largest medical practices in the city for over forty years and for many of them he was on the board of the Toronto Western Hospital, the team doctor for the Toronto Argonauts gridiron football team, served his community as an alderman and school trustee and was a long time member of the United Church and Toronto Masonic Alpha Lodge, A.F. & A.M.

Besides football he had a strong interest in ice hockey (known just as "hockey" in Canada and the US) and baseball. "Hockey" in Australia is known as "Field Hockey" in North America. He mentioned more than once to Mom that he was concerned about me playing hockey as he thought I was too weak and couldn't breathe well enough for that sport. He was almost right. I played defence for a few seasons but eventually I shifted to goal, where, at the age of 22, I finally finished my career without trouble... except for arthritis and constant knee problems which began when I was fourteen and eventually led to two total knee replacement operations in later years.

JW's home in the city was huge and just like him it had many lairs to it. Three stories, brick, three fireplaces, four-car garage, and a pool room the size of Maple Leaf Gardens. Off to the side of the house, but attached were large rooms for his practice. Like him the house had many surprises; for example on the third floor what appeared to be just more of the solid oak panelling that featured throughout the whole house were hidden doors leading to three secret or private rooms (depending on who you were talking to at the time). What went on in there I never found out because the third floor was off limits to all kids and visitors. Twice I can remember creeping up the stairs to find out when I thought it was safe but it was too scary and I descended a hell of a lot faster that I ascended, that's for sure!

Today, I clearly recall over-stuffed leather chairs and big leather furniture in the house and practice rooms, a huge kitchen, dumb waiters, toilets everywhere and the smell of medicines wafting. Outside, because the house was on the corner of one of the main streets in the city, the clang-clang of a TTC streetcar rumbling by would occasionally be brought to your attention, although because the house was built like Fort Knox, it wasn't usually obvious or disturbing.

The Buddha's Nose

He died at that home in his late sixties on August 27, 1949 the result of an auto accident on his way home from the cottage someone told me later.

Here's one I can't collate ... I was seventeen and living at home when he died but I have no memory of his death, funeral or even discussion being held in my house ... nothing! To this day I have no idea about the disposition of his estate. Somebody scored big, but it wasn't Mom. He owned at least five cottages at the lake and three operating farms nearby. Did he have a mistress? Did the Masons receive the spoils? Or were some charity or charities benefactors? I don't know and probably never will.

He was fixated with Chrysler Imperial automobiles and bought a new one each year. He had more than his share of auto accidents, not too surprisingly, because he was a notoriously bad driver. We used to play paper, scissors, rock to escape riding with him...and the loser became the reluctant passenger. When he sat behind the wheel he was as far back in the driver's seat as he could get...his bulk accounted for that. He would grab the steering wheel and hold it like he was beheading two chooks, one hand rigid at twenty after the hour and the other equally tight at twenty to. When it was necessary to turn the car his hands stayed frozen in their same clock positions and only the wheel moved...not his hands! Got it? A Michael Schumaker he wasn't.

The Buddha's Nose

At the beginning of his two week summer vacation period, usually the first of August, he would load up the car with food, clothes, tools, booze...jam-packed.

Then came the three hour drive from Toronto to Round Lake in the Peterboro region of Ontario where, when he arrived, he would park the car at the rear of his cottage, after triple-honking to get people's attention. We were waiting for that impatient noise because we knew it was the signal to promptly make our way to the car, unload, take everything into the cottage and turn on our mind-set that for the next fourteen days we were on call to do his bidding. He would control everything...I mean *everything*, our time, our food, our sleep, our activities even our toilet habits.... no shit!

During the summer, from about the middle of June to the first of August, he might show up when there was a long weekend available. We would never know for sure... but we'd be ready!

Many summers I would arrive first thing when spring ended and it would be just Mabel and me in the cottage, which was okay when she wasn't a miserable tyrant, but I would become very lonely. There were kids to play with most of the time but things would really liven up when Uncle Jack would drive up in his Ford Coupe first thing to open up his cottage for the summer (sometimes with me in tow which was fantastic), then whenever he could on long weekends and for his two weeks holiday, usually in July. I loved Jack and he loved me and we had great times together. He was also an MD and in later years it was his steady hand that was responsible for usually stitching me up after or during a hockey game because in those days we goalies had no face or head protection.

Jack had two good kids around my age and a wife, Edna, who must have been the prototype for The Wicked Witch of the West. I liked her like I liked brand new dog poop on the souls of my bare feet. She was one mean puppy to me, to her kids, to her own father who was a douche bag paedophile and I speak from first-hand knowledge and to Jack, JW and Mabel - especially Mabel.

Because their cottage was next to JW's, can you picture the state of irrationality and bullshit that existed between the women and anyone else who got in between them?... ugly! Oh, the grunting, lower breath mumbling, fixed icy stares and overly-ruddy complexions that went on for all those summers.

Mabel kept a list... yes she did... on any of my transgressions, and turned it over to JW whenever it was called for. She was a whistle-blower that woman. She gave no quarter. For not doing my chores or more serious crimes I would face various and sundry punishments like no boats this week, no swimming, no fishing, confinement to the house for two days, no playing with friends and no liquorice for a week.... now that was the REAL killer!

The Tribal Drums did their job every year and announced to the folks around that lake that it was JW's birthday soon, and they came.... dozens of them, with presents, booze and good wishes. I know there was liquor because every summer at that time we young kids were told in no uncertain terms to NEVER drink what the grown-ups drank or we would be drowned, hung, quartered or all the above. Naturally that was a red flag to a bull and I tried to guzzle as many nips as I could get away with before I got caught or pissed, whichever came first.

The party was always a roaring success... twenty or so people sitting on each side of a long make-shift table stretched down the wharf or dock towards the end and the quietly lapping water on three sides. Many boats moored there from the folks who came from all around the lake. By the end of the day you can imagine what happened. Reasonably regulated mayhem that's what... a warm day, buckets of cold beer, expensive liquor and devil-may-care-ness suggested only one conclusion. And JW sat facing the cottage at the end of the dock like a pontificating Buddha... like the conductor of a completely out of tune symphony orchestra of disrepute... overseeing a table heaped high of outrageously good food and constantly topped-up wine goblets, because he would never settle for anything less, at any time. They were great parties while they lasted. Cleaning up after wasn't much fun though. In those days the females did all the preparation, serving and straightening up while the males did nothing but get more pissed and the kids did what they were told to do.... mostly.

At the rear of the cottage, just before you came to the single lane dirt road that passed by, he built what was called an ice shed; well he had someone build it. It was constructed entirely of logs; front, sides and roof... no windows and just one extra wide door with a substantial lock. It was about six and a half feet high and maybe six feet by ten feet of space. Over the shed he had built, what we would call today a car port, made of wood. This was a protective device against the weather. Inside the shed he had tons of sawdust shovelled into place so that ice squares or blocks ranging from twenty pounds to fifty pounds could be piled on top of each other and nestled away in the protective sawdust and kept reasonably well frozen for when needed. That was the upside!

The downside was that there was no light, it was always freezing cold and all kinds of creatures decided it was a perfect place to come to get away from it all.... and multiply with sustained vigour.

To be locked in the Ice Shed for punishment for a sizeable crime and do the time was the ultimate prison for some of us to deal with. I can only now remember it happened to me twice but I can't recall what I did to deserve it. It was the absolute scare though... and I do hold on to it today! Cold, deadly quiet, things moving around me... oh shit, there's something climbing up my bare leg now!!

One of my regular chores was to go to the ice shed with my trusty little all wooden wagon and a set of large heavy tongs and bring back to Mabel a block or two of ice to be placed in the ice box. I hated the ice shed...and still do!

JW loved to fish and that was too bad for me. He'd wake me by the usual bed-shaking method very early (still dark) and the day would begin. I would load the boat with whatever he felt was necessary.... fuel, fishing gear, bait, sun tan lotion, which was usually a bottle of baby oil with a few drops of iodine added, a life preserver for me (he never wore one), sandwiches, thermoses...especially the blue one, hats, buckets, knives and a positive attitude. I learned early on that a positive attitude caught fish... yes I did!

When we set out I would be sitting as far forward as I could get and JW would be operating the motor. Even though he sat as far forward as he could while still steering his bulk made the made the bow of the boat rise so that it was half out of the water and the faster he would go, the higher was the rise. I was always fascinated, while at the same time shit-scared, that at any moment the water that was lapping the rear area would soon come in and the expected baling and fear inside me would explode. As the lapping got stronger over the gunnels and more threatening he would apparently see my change of colour to a chalk white. That was his clue: 'ted, if the boat goes under I won't worry 'cause I know you'll save me...right?". Remember, he never wore a life jacket and he couldn't swim as stroke, or could he?.... oh my!

Our fishing expositions were always pretty much the same: first thing in the morning right across the lake to certain bar about 200 meters from the shore where the small mouth bass and the colourful perch lived together most of the year. The water was deep there but JW taught me how to drop my line to the bottom and then bring it up a few feet... and wait. During this still-fishing exercise at some point he would decide to stretch and so up he would get with unsteady legs, still holding on to his rod, and the poor boat would moan and groan and creek as he shifted position. I kept praying that he would not get a strike while he was standing there because I saw the final results as horrific...for him and for me. Thankfully the bass must have understood my dilemma and never chose to test his balance.

The final part of the day (four or five hours actually) was always trolling for Muskies. They were large, long, sleek fighters usually about four feet of raw power. Often they'd be found in the deeper parts of the lake, more in the middle. When one hit all hell broke loose. JW would have to shift seats so that he was now facing the rear of the boat on either side of the motor.

"I'm gonna die now, I know it."

But I didn't. The water flowed in, the boat screamed out its dislike of the circumstances, and I sat petrified while he landed the fish. That night, after I had cleaned and filleted it, Mabel cooked it and I rejoiced in seeing another day of life.

Stone the Crows

"Stone the Crows."

Each time I hear that expression today, yesterday immediately becomes right now...

There were a number of large trees of some kind beside the cottage. Each year they would be inhabited by various and sundry crows and ravens. JW hated them with a passion because they crapped everywhere, were noisy and often decided to dive bomb anyone they chose. I and a couple of the other kids in the area use to make new, stronger slingshots each summer in order to get into new and stronger trouble each year. Of course I had great success without fail.

One year when I was seven or eight JW saw my slingshot and came up with a plan.

"Ted, I'm leaving today but tomorrow morning when you get up I want you to take your slingshot out to the trees around the cottage and see how many crows you can hit and kill. For everyone you kill I'll pay you twenty cents. As you kill them put them in a bag and put the bag in the ice shed and the next time I'm down here we'll take out the bag and count how many twenty cent coins I will owe you, ok?"

"Yes sir"

"Good, start tomorrow!"

Hoist with my own petard.

I hit a couple that day but because I was shooting with much reduced power on purpose it only seemed to sting them...certainly not knock them off their perch. I didn't want to kill them, or even hurt them for that matter. I didn't like to kill things then and I still don't.

The proverbial hit the fan when JW came back a few weeks later and found no bag in the ice shed. When the anger had subsided the result was ever-imprinted. That same day he got out the single shot Remington and off we went to a field nearby and with bottles and tin cans in tow my education in shooting began in earnest. I don't know how long we were there that day but a couple of hours is probably about right.

When we got back he had me stand under the tree and start firing. I recall now that Mabel ran out in anger at him doing this to a child. He stopped me and I was free until another day. Fortunately for me that "another day" never came!

Swimming

JW had an obvious soft spot for my mom, Lois. I suspect he had great plans for her all along... until she meant Eddie Heaton, that is. She was eighteen when she got pregnant and Eddie was 32, a reprobate, lazy lout and no goodnik, at least that was how JW saw it. Lois had just returned from Paris after two years of finishing school and "POW" preggers.

I never saw JW swim: as a matter of fact I never saw him above his waist in the water but he demanded that everyone else learn to swim. He loved watching Lois swim with her athletic body and winning smile. He knew she had been a successful basketball player and equally competent at fencing, but as a swimmer, outstanding!

Most summers, when Lois would come to the cottage for a week or so to check on her son, she would make sure that she swam over to the other side of the lake, about three miles away and sometimes back again. JW was proud as punch, so was I... but Mabel, she just grunted.

Miss Newton

Miss Newton was my Grade Five teacher and I loved her and wanted to marry her and rescue her from it all. In retrospect I see that this was the beginning of my deep-seated need and desire to 'save" women ... remove them from their lesser world into a freer and fresher better world...I would be their salvation. I was about eleven and she was my first true love ... oooeee, I loved that girl!!

One winter's day for whatever reason I can't recall now she asked me to bring something over to her house not far from mine. When I arrived at her door it had been snowing all day, it was dark and the street lights glistened and the street was hushed as the snow muffled the tire noises. I carried something but can't remember what...maybe it was my heart in a basket because I had loved her all year by then. I rang the bell. The outside light went on, the door opened and there she was in all her beauty. She was gorgeous! She wore a thin, thin see-through nightgown and the light in the house behind her accented the scene incredibly. I couldn't move. I couldn't talk. I could only stare in awe.

With a sultry voice she asked me in but I whispered no thankyou as my parents expected me to come right back. She smiled an understanding grin, thanked me, closed the door and I stood there, transfixed for about three hours...well, maybe three minutes but it seemed like three hours.

The Green Dragon Gang

Later in the year, as Spring made its presence known, I had just left Miss Newton's class one day on my way home...a distance of about fifteen minutes or so... and was off the school property minding my own business when I sensed a commotion behind me.

The Buddha's Nose

There were five of them, big guys, teenagers. Even though they were about 50 yards away and had masks on I knew who they were...THE GREEN DRAGON GANG....because lots of kids in my school had been terrorized by them in the past for a couple of years or so. They scared old people and girls and women and disabled folks. They stole, damaged cars and houses and sometimes were physically abusive, especially to teenage girls. The cops never seemed to be able to stop them. No one seemed to know who they were.

On this particular day I was their target... not because I did anything to them but just because I was there, I guess.

They began to trot slowly towards me. I turned away and started the after-burners. Trouble was I had very little "burners" and my "after" was almost all gone already. I had been sick a lot that winter and was weak and the result was that Toby the Turtle could have beaten me in a ten yard sprint. But I ran as fast as I could and they came after me yelling and making threatening gestures as three of them flew past me faster than the wind.

They stopped about twenty feet in front of me, three facing me and two behind me.

Caged me up without touching me. They yelled, swore at me, told me what they were going to do to me. I cried and they laughed. The more they laughed the more I cried, the more I cried the more they laughed. People could see what was happening but no one did anything about it, I think they thought it was funny. Bastards!

The Buddha's Nose

Finally they opened up and let me through. They told me to run and I did. They followed but never with the intent of catching me. They chased me right home almost to my door, told my they'd see me tomorrow and left.

When I got inside and mom saw my state she was shaken. When I told her it was the Green Dragon Gang I thought I saw some fear in her, which was most unusual.

The next day was Friday and mom kept me home from school so I had the weekend to recuperate. On Monday I felt pretty good but I missed dad who was away on business, as usual.

When I got into class I told Miss Newton about the gang and she was sincerely concerned for my health and well being and said she would call my parents and talk to them about this matter. That made me feel better....but not for long because after school the same thing happened again. They were waiting for me at the same spot but this time they just trotted behind me all the way home without a sound...nothing, zilch, nada. In many ways that was more scary than the other treatment they gave me, but I learned that day how loud silence can be!!

Right up to the door again. I was beside myself when I entered the house. I was sick and mom spotted that right away. She called JW and talked to him for a few moments, hung up came back to me and told me not to worry Grandad was going to look after the whole thing tomorrow but he would come and see me tonight. He did. We talked and he left. He told mom not to worry, he would fix it and she believed him and told me so.

The Buddha's Nose

The next afternoon as I came out of school surprise of all surprises there was JW waiting for me to take me home in his hot rod. When we got into the house he gathered mom and I together and made the following statement: "The Green Dragon Gang will never bother you again, not today, not tomorrow, not ever." That was all he said.

From that day to this I never heard another word about the Green Dragon Gang.... nor did anyone else as far as I know. That was a perfect example of JW's power!

Poison Ivy

Each summer part of my routine was to spend time at one or more of JW's farms. It was a no-debate situation. Mabel made the arrangements with the tenants and that was that. Well the first year I went to the farm they had me searching for berries... especially wild raspberries, which I love to this day... and blueberries. Knowing no better and being given no direct instructions, and having found them before, I set out for the closest potential under growth around the area to get the picking job done. It was two years later that two and two made four and the grownups finally figured out that it was that first year when I contracted poison ivy originally. I say "originally" because after the condition re-visited me each year for seven long and extremely embarrassing ones I became a world-wide expert in learning how *not* to scratch and how to handle bullying.

Mom's medical upbringing, as well as her nursing credentials certainly helped our family, no doubt. But sometimes it was a problem. Before you could say "Bob's

Your Uncle" the poison ivy had spread up my legs into my hair and all over my body.... scratching made sure of that! Geez, I'm scratching now as I remember.

As soon as she saw the blisters she knew what it was and out came the calamine lotion and cotton buds. That left the skin with large blotches of white over a highly tanned body...outlined and grossly noticeable like the proverbial dog's balls!

But worse was to come! When school started around the first of September the PI was still there requiring the lotion and bandaging wherever possible to stop me scratching. But the bandages on the legs kept slipping and uncovering the horrible-looking blisters some of which were busting and re-infecting. Her solution? Bandage the legs again and cover the bandage to the knees with my school stockings and under them with *women's silk stockings* up under my short pants and kept in place with female garters. I'm sure you've got the picture and if you haven't then you're just simply not taking this description seriously enough. It's true! If you listen carefully you may still be able to see and hear the bullying at school and on the way to and from home that went on every day for weeks on end.... I think it's still in the ethers.

She made sure that a couple of my friends agreed to walk with me to school each day... about thirty minutes one way... and paid them something for their efforts. When I think of it now, she should have paid ME!

The Buddha's Nose

Bees and Wasps and Honey Buckets

One of my occasional chores at the cottage was to drive away families of bees and or wasps. Usually I did that with a long-handled broom because the beasts were situated high up in the eaves. They got really pissed off at the interruption and would dive bomb me regularly, even days later ... I was absolutely sure they had a vivid memory of retribution. I used to like to watch Uncle Jack high up on a ladder clean them out of his place with a blow torch. It was a kind of Russian roulette as to whether he would get those creatures done and dusted before he burned his cottage to the ground ... even money bet.

And now to my worst chore at the cottage...the Honey Bucket. Picture this: you dig a large four foot wide by three feet deep hole in the ground about 40 feet away from the main building, place two large metal buckets in the hole beside each other, cover the area with copious sprinklings of lime, construct a wooden side-by-side two seater with splinters, structure a wooden four-sided building, big enough to be cramped space for all but the littlest, add a leaky roof and a door that locked only some of the time, no light, plenty of room for spiders, bees, wasps, snakes and other animals with peculiar eating habits ... and you've got the typical cottage outhouse of the day.

As the buckets filled up they would have to be lifted out of their spot, transported to either another hole that had been newly dug and the contents dropped into there and covered up immediately, or take the contents and spread it to help gardens grow… they called it fertilizer… I called it SHIT!

I don't remember how many times a summer we had to empty the honey buckets but I DO recall that the day after the Birthday party was the one day in the year that all of us wanted to be out fishing or somewhere from the earliest of the day to the darkest of the night in hope that we could avoid the call because who ever was left hangin' around did the job that day for sure.

The Bear

After apparently graduating from destroying dozens of beer bottles and crows with my trustee 22 calibre Remington rifle, JW had decided one day that it was time for me, at about the age of nine to understand the real call of mother nature….**The Great White Hunter.**

Not far from the cottage was a large empty field backed up by a steep rugged hill which, when you reached the top, led to one of JW's many farms in the area. He knew the land and its inhabitants very well and often expressed a real concern about the number of bears that appeared in the vicinity.

From his point of view they were a physical threat to all and sundry and they also killed farm animals and raided kitchens in the vicinity… they were scoundrels, thieves and killers… and they were in the process of multiplying at an unacceptable rate given their propensity for destruction. That was his theory!

The Buddha's Nose

One very early still dark morning in August he woke me in his usual charming manner...two or three rough shakes of the bed, not the sheet or pillows, the bed. "Gitup!!"

No sooner had I staggered into the kitchen for my usual cup of hot chocolate, toasted crumpets with honey and porridge when he made the announcement, and my life was about to change forever and ever amen.

To Grandma Mabel his wife, although you would be forgiven if you said you didn't know her name, because I can never recall ever hearing him call her by name... or vice versa for that matter. There were just a series of grunts exchanged, or so it seemed to me then...and now as I think back grunting was what he did a lot of. She was a good grunter too, but why wouldn't she be? But he didn't need to do much more than that because he had control. I remember as I write this that he would often say in his larger than life, barrel-chested, basso profundo, no nonsense manner of speaking, "I believe there are two ways of doing things, my way or my way."

I don't remember anyone ever laughing when he said that...especially him!

But back to the announcement.

"Today Ted and I are going bear hunting and we'll be back before noon."

Mabel grunted her usual reply that she had heard what was said and with that guttural sound she squeezed out conveyed the clear message that she didn't give a shit anyway. An amazing communication skill, grunting!

The Buddha's Nose

I heard him too, but the impact wasn't there then... that followed some time later.

He loaded us into his new pet Chrysler Imperial, along with a 22 rifle, a double barrel shotgun, a couple of pistols and enough ammunition to adequately defend all of northern Canada and Alaska should WW Three ever break out. He also had a few thermoses filled with things like hot coffee, water and some sort of interesting drink, which in later years I recognised its smell as that of good quality rum. He even had a few pots and pans and wooden-handled spoons as well. The night before, Mabel had apparently made a wide range of sandwiches to feed the Great White Hunters on their upcoming safari.

We drove around the eastern side of the lake until he found the precise inland spot he had in mind... I had the feeling then that he had checked the place out more than once and knew exactly where he wanted to go.... "My way or my way."

We parked off to the side of the single lane washboard road. I unloaded everything and was told where to put it all, which I did, in neat little mounds.

In front of where we had our supplies was a very large old tree that had fallen down flat of its own accord or had been hit by lightning. It was lying parallel to the side of the road about twenty yards from its shoulder. A man could lie behind it on the ground and not be seen from across the field. Most men that is, but not JW. To hide him would require a stacked small forest of giant redwoods.

The Buddha's Nose

By now it's about 8am and the weather is warming up already. August in that part of Canada gets quite hot early in the day and cools down nicely as the sun dies.

He helps himself to a swig of coffee from a brown thermos and follows that up with a couple of gobbles of some of that other juice in the blue thermos. He seems happy. As for me, I'm just plain confused. We both have a couple of sandwiches, some water and he has more coffee and some of that other stuff. He laughs at something and I laugh with him...I'm happy that he's happy.

He pulls out his watch fob, sees it's after 9 am and decides it's time. He sits on top of the log and beckons me to join him facing away from the road.

"Ted, do you see where my finger is pointing about 150 yards across the meadow to where there is a large clump of foliage.... trees and bushes.... just as the hill begins to climb upwards from the field?"

"Yes sir."

"Good, now in that clump of bushes and trees I think there is a home in there that momma and poppa bear live at with three or four of their children. Today we're going to get rid of some of those bears because they are very dangerous to us and they are now coming around the cottage and the farms looking for food and could hurt or kill us. Do you understand?"

"Yes sir."

"Right, in a minute we're going to see if we can wake those pesky bears up if they are there in the first place. And the way we'll do that, is you and I will go around to the front of this tree and each of us will take a pot and spoon and bang and yell and make noise until they come out to see who's here. Then, when they see us they'll come towards us across the field because they will be protecting their cubs and they'll be mad."

I was following along ok up until now as the total point of all this had not yet settled on my young brain.

"When they get close enough we'll shoot them, you with your Remington and me with my shotgun."

Now I got the whole picture in my head and years later, when I had the bejeezus scared out of me from the shower scene in Psycho, I realised that I had had that feeling of fear once before.... behind a fallen tree near Round Lake when I was ordered to shoot to kill.... and that's what it was, no doubt about it. I'm just saying.

"Do you understand?"

"Yes sir."

He had another guzzle or two from the blue thermos, and smiled and of course so did I.

"Okay, now load your gun, place your ammunition by your right side, take one of those pots and spoons and stand in front of the log facing that space over there and I'll do the same."

He did and we did. I was curious, a bit scared but not too much, the testosterone was just starting to twitch a little bit in me by then and I've often wondered since if that day was the beginning or the ending of something... I don't know!

The festivities started with him shooting a few shots from his pistols at the target area in general but nothing seemed to happen. Next, the pot serenade began. Fortunately there were no people anywhere close to us because if there had been they would have probably thought that the world was ending. Before long, for one of us at least, it was!

I have often wished I had a picture of the scene, JW and me standing in front of the fallen log creating god-awful noise as well as making ourselves visible to who or whatever might be around. Fools rush in don't they?

Then it happened... she seemed to crash through the underbrush, into the open space and faced us from across the meadow. I saw her growl, "You motherfuckers" or something similar. She appeared to be very, very big and cumbersome as she made her way warily towards us, one heavy paw after another. As she got closer each step seemed like a minor aftershock... the earth quakes didn't really begin till she was much nearer and madder.

"Alright Ted, get behind the log and aim for her head with your first shot, I'll tell you when. If it doesn't stop her load and fire again."

If it doesn't stop her?... what is he saying to me? I wish I wasn't here. I wish I was back home in Toronto with my parents and friends. I wish I was back at the cottage. She's still coming, thump, thump, thump. She's drooling now I can see it.

"Okay Ted, she's about fifty yards away, get ready to fire when I say shoot. Remember, aim for her head."

The only thing shaking more than my hands was the rest of me... I shook all over. My bowels would have turned inside out if I had thought about them, but I was way too scared to worry about a shitty little thing like that.

"Now Ted, SHOOT!" he commanded.

I steadied my elbows on the log like JW had shown me dozens of times in the past. I aimed.

"Deep breath, hold it, squeeze the trigger softly," he directed me. "Do it my way or do it my way," I could almost hear him say.

The shot hit her on the side of her neck. It seemed to surprise her more than hurt her, but she yelled a call of anger and reared up to her full height. She seemed to be so high up, higher than the sky, higher than Jack in the Beanstalk, higher than God's living room, higher than the moon, higher than a New Years Eve party at King's Cross... she was enormous and really, really pissed.

She came down onto all fours while I was trying to desperately reload but I couldn't find the slot for the bullet, well I could find it but I couldn't hold it still, or so it seemed.

She was twenty steps away from us... no more, and still coming, filled with rage, when JW aimed the shotgun and I heard the two barrels empty at almost the same time. She dropped within maybe ten feet distance to the log. I could see she was still breathing when JW went cautiously around the side of the log with his pistol's safety off and standing close by shot her in the left side of the brain. I think she was a good mother who cared about her brood and paid the ultimate price for her love.

Oh my, just telling the story brings it all back with such a rush.

The Buddha's Nose

A few days later I went home to Toronto without ever finding out what finally happened to the bear's family. I never heard another word about it and the next summer when I asked Mabel what happened all I got was a disdainful grunt... no surprises there!

The Other Side

JW was a man of distinction, no doubt about it. He had all the negative and positive aspects to his personality that I have explored herein, but he had something else as well ... he was a healer who cared about mankind and suffered fools badly and I think in his own way he was also a man of God who believed in something mysterious far beyond us. As I've said before, he was a life-saver! I know I'm still here primarily because of him.

From the age of seven until about twelve I had pneumonia and pleurisy three times... the first two before penicillin. I saw the light at the end of the tunnel twice that I can recall and I still remember today the searing pain in my sides with each breath I took. It was JW who looked after me with regular visits to the house during the deeply urgent days of sickness, telephone calls to Mom and even phone calls to the local chemist to send certain prescriptions over to her immediately, regardless of the time or the day. They'd get there presto-pronto too.

After my third bout of the disease JW made a frightening recommendation to Mom. One that must have had serious consequences all around.

The Buddha's Nose

To set the stage: ever since JW found out that Ed Heaton had stolen his beautiful, precious, eighteen year old daughter in the middle of the night and then gotten her pregnant and given her only a middle class life at best, when she should have had it all, the hate between the two men was rampant. They stayed out of each other's way for years and years and didn't even use each other's name any more than was absolutely necessary. I give Mom credit for the family co-ordination capabilities she most surely must have shown to hold it all together. I think I may have played a part in her plan as well.

That day JW told his daughter that it was his belief that his grandson was probably fatally unwell and unless he had his left lung removed completely it would collapse sooner rather than later and the boy would die... no mincing of words, I'm sure.

With her medical background Mom may have taken it reasonably well, but inside the churning must have been enormous. She may have even been in shock. She told her father that she'd talk with Ed that night and let JW know the decision tomorrow, as time was of the essence.

When Ed returned from work that evening she would have patiently waited until he had consumed his regular second glass of Scotch down in his den, in his relaxing chair listening to the news on CBC Radio Canada. Then she told him JW's recommendation. I know because she eventually discussed that night and subsequent nights and days in vivid detail with me in later years and even used the language that flew that night as well…. most unlike any lady of the times… especially her.

"What?" Ed yelled and jumped out of his chair, hands on hips, face beet red. "Do you think I would ever allow that bastard to slice open a kid of mine? You tell that fucker tomorrow morning to stay away from my boy or I'll come over there and destroy him. Not one finger on the kid, do you get it?"

She got it!

I don't know what she told her dad the next day (she wouldn't be specific with me about that) but whatever it was it solved the difficulty. Although soon it opened up a whole new series of other problems for me when Dad decided to take me to the inhalation hospital. What happened to me there I have outlined in another chapter of this book.

Grandad saved my life twice for sure and maybe as much as three times. He also taught me to fish, operate a motor boat, row properly and shoot, as well as how to behead a chook, milk a cow, ride a horse, pick crab apples, hunt for raspberries and rabbits, stay away from rattle snakes and red back spiders and obey my elders.

Maybe, just maybe he wasn't the bastard I thought he was all these years!

Irving Says

"Writing is a great therapy."

How often has that passed by me over the years? I've seen and heard the idea expressed as a possible tool of self enlightenment many times but I must admit that to me it was basically a "new age" philosophy for academics. Till now!

Now writing is extremely therapeutic for me not just a workable philosophy. For example, my last sentence above where I question JW's "bastardness" is a case in point. I have accused him in perpetuity of a myriad of my pain, hurt, personality struggles, fears, anxieties and sometimes sleepless nights. All of which is probably fair and deserving. But the other side counter-balances it all.

I see now that he was in love with me in his own way and how he chose to show it was his way too.

I forgive what needs forgiving, acknowledge what needs acknowledging, respect his being him, and here and now say with love: Goodnight JW, sleep well Grampa...sorry I never sat on your knee! Next time maybe. And thankyou!

Chapter Eight - Short

Lois Mabel Heaton, nicknamed 'Short.' As I look back she was perhaps the most influential Authority Figure of my life.

She received her nickname from me as soon as I was taller than her. Jon hadn't reached the required height yet but he used the name anyway because that seemed to make Mom upset and that was part of our quest in life but we never thought of it as being mean or evil, just fun.

She was a natural athlete and involved in many sports at higher levels. Swimming long and short distances, was something she pursued well up into her seventies. She came from a family of medical people, her father, brother, uncle, cousins and so on. And it was on the cards that when she returned to Toronto from Paris where she was finishing her education, she would become a registered nurse. But as soon as she was back, love and intrigue got in the way of the best laid plans. Well, best plans; laid was another matter altogether. Fast Eddie and Short eloped when she was eighteen and he was 32... she was also pregnant and her daddy, JW was not a happy man. That's the understatement of the century!

Through her I learned the ways, means and reasons for social graces like etiquette and good manners, how to crochet and knit, how to swim, the value of good music, why ballet and opera were important, that all people were not equal: and that discrimination was important, so were the right kind of friends; be good to those below you on the social ladder; people are judged by what they own and display and it's not necessary to love all the members of your immediate family if you don't want to.

Some of the above that I learned I discarded long ago, even things like what size fork goes closest to the plate, but some engrams have stayed with me and have been of value to me and my kids, I think. At least I hope so.

She loved her brother Jack, but not so much her sister Beryl, who was the black sheep of the family, until I came along, that is. I finally took over that mantle, unopposed. Although it can certainly be said that Fast Eddie definitely held a place of consequence with Short's miserable bastard of a father and inconsequential mother, but I covered all the bases on both sides of the family ledger.

When I needed money as a youngster and later as an adult (I was going to say as a grown up, but I realise I'm not there yet....long way to go, mate) I went to Short. If it was just a few bucks she would loan it to me, but if it was hundreds or thousands she would become my intermediary with Fast Eddie. She and I had learned much earlier that there was much more chance of success this way, than me going directly to him and then have to deal with the inquisition which was inevitable. The system worked pretty well for us all I think.

I've been an orphan from sometime in 1986 but

interestingly, I still feel their presence and remember some of the good, bad and ugly that was part of just plain living with them and Jon. Whether I was living in Toronto, Sydney, Hong Kong, London or LA, I always called them on New Year's Eve.... it was a ritual of respect and love from me to them. Small things matter!

Mom enjoyed playing the piano, painting pictures, collecting antiques, silverware, jewellery, mink and fox stoles and coats, and impressive friends. It was important for her to be able to tell all and sundry that this girl friend of hers was a top soprano of renown or that this one played piano with the Boston Symphony. Those two women were friends of hers all her adult life and whatever the bond was between them it certainly withstood the test of time.

Short lived with some interesting idiosyncrasies, which were uniquely her. For example, each time I introduced her to a new lady in my life it wouldn't take very long before my relationship with the latest love would be in trouble because Mom would decide to give her a 'present' on her birthday, Christmas, St Swithin's Day or just because it was time to show her displeasure with my choice. Trouble my friend, trouble, right there in River City!!

One of her habits of disrespect was to go to some god forsaken place in the bowels of the city where there was a walk-up, third storey, second hand fur shop and negotiate with the owner, whom she knew from previous visits there, to buy a grossly second hand raggedy fox stole that was probably stored away downstairs in the furnace room of the building a century ago. And the resident mice played bridge on it.

She'd bring it home, wrap it in some cheap paper or just present it on a regular clothes hanger...hanging there drooping, all forlorn! Needless to say it would be received with wide-eyed awe, a furtive glance towards me (who would be sure to be looking somewhere else at the time) a pleasant thankyou from the recipient. The show of good manners would last until we got to the car and then the screen would come down and the shit would hit the fan.

It happened to them all so finally I saw what was going on and the message that she was giving which was 'You're nowhere good enough for my darling son ...piss off.'

Sometimes she was right!

It was terribly embarrassing for both my lady and me but the system never faltered, year after year after year.

As far back as I can recall Mom was a hypochondriac of the first water. She loaded up on so many pills that the house was slanted. Some I understood but most I didn't.

There were many dichotomies with her but one of the best was the way she treated hired help. They all knew she was the Queen of the Manor and she dealt with them as you would expect a Queen would with her servants. And yet they loved her and usually kept in touch long after their work there was through. She gave them stoles sometimes too... or cracked bric-a-bracs... used clothing or occasionally tickets to some minor concert.

Short had a persona that demanded attention, and she got it. My ability to negotiate comes directly from her because I often attended a 'stole-buying' exhibition or something similar (especially used jewellery, art work, antiques, dinner ware) and picked up on her tone of voice, use of the language, eye contact, dress sense (usually one of her good Mink stoles would come out of moth balls for the contest) and most of all her preparation. She always prepared first and foremost before she went on her excursions for used silver plates or other silver goodies too numerous to mention now.

I loved my Mom a lot and learned early on to accept her strangeness as well as her consistent love and care for me, Dad and Jon. Sometimes she drove me absolutely nuts. I would never have traded her!

A man who has been the favourite of his mother keeps for life the feeling of a conqueror....Sigmund Freud

Irving Says

If you wish, think about your mother.

How influential was your Mother in the process of you growing up?

What lessons did you learn from her that are still with you today?

What have you transferred from your Mother's brain to your kids?

The Buddha's Nose

What mistakes did your Mom make and how have they affected you?

What is the greatest legacy Mom has, or will, leave you with?

What was the major on-going problem you had or have with Mom?

What do you respect the most about Mom?

If you could say just ONE sentence to Mom right now, what would it be?

Chapter Nine - Atavism

ATAVISM; *from the Latin Atavus meaning 'Ancestor'*

I'm going to take some time now to deal with what to me is an extremely important subject, because it answers so many questions about the past and the future. The clearer the subject, the larger the span of possibilities exists to 'know thyself.' Stick with me.

The human condition is always connected and influenced by its most ancient of history

"Phylogenics is the development and history of the genetic makeup of all living things brought to the current status. Phylogenic acquisitions are these archaic expressions of early racial experiences which we inherit. The mass of these ancient racial and psychic acquisitions contribute to the individual unconsciousness."

Douglas Baker

Traditional psychiatry maintains that Atavism is: a genetic throwback in which a characteristic from within that family reappears after being absent for some generations ...

"The way in which the past influences the present

structure." I have no problem with that.... as far as it goes, but it doesn't go nearly far enough.

I believe that there is much, much more to atavism than that, Atavism also means that **features from past lives surface...strange, peculiar psychological features that may be pathological or even sexual-pathological. Features appear from previous lives or personal genetics.**

For example, some people will manifest a particular disease that has hardly ever been seen within that family group. And yet, one of the older members of the family will remark that they remember their grandfather had the same kind of sickness, but they haven't seen or heard of it since, within their own line of genetics ... therefore, it's a condition that suddenly manifests again ... up from the depths of nowhere.

It's as if some psychological feature from the past knocks on the door of the Now and demands to be allowed to enter into life again, at the level of this generation. And that psychological entity becomes the cause of an immune system deficiency, which, in its turn, leads to the physical condition from the family's past ... the condition that we call sickness or disease.

In other words we are looking at the Unconscious... either the Collective or the Individual Unconscious. In esoteric terms these are referred to as Akashic Records.

By understanding the concept behind Atavism we need to ponder, meditate and consider carefully the condition we are presented with. And the more knowledge we have in our possession, the more reliable will be our estimate of the situation that an individual has immersed himself or herself in.

Transgenderism may be something in a particular family that has not been seen or experienced since good old uncle Jack's father's father was shown to be a cross-dresser. And the family has ever since made believe that the old man didn't even really exist. Stories have been developed over the years to hide the truth from all and sundry. But, that old man's great-grandson has just "come out of the closet," as we call it. And the shock to the family is intense! How did he become gay? Was he always gay? Or is this something he has "learned" to enjoy? Or is it much deeper? Or is this his way of simply rebelling against his parents and grandparents? And what does he mean by, 'I'm in the wrong body?' And so goes the conjecture within the family clan.

Sometimes the condition may be much more dangerous and pathological, such as perhaps the Port Arthur killer and his strange and weird ways that many saw, but most dismissed as simply "peculiar."

Other times it can be more along the lines of the bizarre, with traits that appear to have no validity within that particular family.

But we must always be clearly and consciously aware of a very important esoteric aphorism: **the human condition is always connected and influenced by its most ancient of history.**

The Buddha's Nose

Even though we are now in a concrete, solidified physical appearance, this is simply a present manifestation of the outcome of a series of events in the deepest past that we originally moved around in. Therefore we are constantly and regularly impinged upon by those same forces, as they are still most latent and most able to affect us often.

From the physical point, for example, I'm satisfied that we were once etheric in nature and have kept that etheric body with us as we have materialised. Going further back, we were at one stage a mental entity only ... then an astral entity ... then etheric. I believe that in the earliest days of Lemuria, when the human began to solidify, it was the aspect of sexuality that first manifested. Later, in the time of Atlantis, it was emotions, feelings, sensations that grew into our very being. Therefore, we can expect antiquated primordial energies and forces that we are linked to, from time immemorial to the present day, to surface in us ... usually, when we would least expect such a thing to occur. Check me out when you can.

We must always be well aware of the very basic esoteric fact that all the time these aspects of the human aura, or levels or principles of man, are active within and around us. And by their very virtue, they are in touch with your past and mine, and that link is an active and impressionistic part of what we see in the physical you or me.

How can this thing of atavism exist? It hinges on deposits of energy that we have left behind us through those dozens and dozens of lives that we have lived on this planet, as part of the process of our individual soul's development.

The Buddha's Nose

We are today the magnets for the attraction of minute atomic-like bulbs of personal history that we call Permanent Atoms or Psychogenes. The more we understand about the doctrine of the Permanent Atoms or Psychogenes, the more we can appreciate the fact that we are historical beings of ancient origin who are proceeding along this track of two-fold evolution: that is to say, the evolution of the soul and the evolution of the physical body, the emotions, the intellect and the spirit.

When we die in the physical sense, we don't just take off and leave a vacuum where once we existed. Everything lives within something else.

We leave behind us a nodal point, or region, that emits radiating forces through its own inherent capabilities.

For example, if we have written a song that has come to the attention of friends or family, whenever that song is played or sung, there we are ... we have been pulled to that location through the thoughts and feelings of those in the room ... and we become, as it were, alive again, at least for a few seconds or minutes as the thoughts of us are conjured up in those in attendance. The consciousness that comes with the experience is something that can be felt again ... perhaps as much as four or five lives later.

When we study sections of Esoteric Psychology such as esoteric healing, the richness of it all supplies us with explanations, directions, possibilities and potentialities that without our knowledge would be unrealistic to assume we could deal with. Obviously, orthodox medicine does not and would not, at least at this point, be able to consider a proposition like atavism as being valid or reasonable, or possible. Although there are encouraging signs of serious changes of thinking by many in the medical fraternity.

 Some of the workings of Atavism:

Philippus Aureolus Theophrastus Bombastus Paracelsus von Hohenheim was born about 1490 and lived into his late 40s or early 50s. He was a physician of great influence and an esotericist of great power and knowledge. He taught that true knowledge came from two distinct ways and methods, Intuition and Experience. He believed that the purpose of intuition was to reveal certain basic issues and concepts that were then proven by one's personal experiences. And, this intuition, and the experiences that surround it, could be either related to the here and now, or could be the result of past lives, and that atavistic tendencies played a part in the development and understanding of the human.

Apparently Paracelsus was one of the past lives of the renowned medical doctor, surgeon and metaphysician, Douglas Baker. This is common knowledge to many, but was never more brought to the fore than when he decided, a few years ago, to put Paracelsus's life on full length film, which he produced, wrote and acted in. At the same time he wrote a book on the subject of Paracelsus that has become something of a standard research vehicle for people interested in that particular life.

Paracelsus's life was in many ways an absolute parallel to that of Douglas. They were both treated with the exact same disdain by their fellow doctors for their outlandish behaviour and beliefs. The difference was that Douglas eventually won many of his detractors over to his side, where as Paracelsus was pushed over a cliff to his immediate death, by his peers who feared him with the passions that existed in those days towards ignorance of the mystical.

Paracelsus' name "Bombastus" was Greek for pretentious, high-falutin', or inflated speaking, one who has excessive confidence in themselves and their material. It was an accusation that was levelled at Paracelsus often and with great rancor and disdain. The bombastic attitude that we sometimes see in certain people was named after Paracelsus himself.

Douglas tells a story on himself. He explained that one of his problems in earlier life was that he had this upsurging of bombast within him that manifested itself as great rising of anger whenever he was talked down to. He would meet this situation with an enormous upsurge of force to answer back in the most indelicate of ways possible.

This condition was so unique that there was no sign of any kind of this peculiar personality trait existing in any part of his life that he could find. There was nothing to suggest that, as far back as he could check on realistically, any similar kind of trait was evident in his family. But he shared it with Paracelsus ... it was an atavistic personality trait from a past life, not family oriented.

Each of us has some, or in some cases many, atavistic personality traits that come from either source ... past family connections, or past life experiences.

Now to another example for your consideration:

The Buddha's Nose

When was the last time that you entered a room, either in real life or in dream state, that was so very familiar to you. The people, the conversation, the situation ... all of it was so real that there was no doubt that you have had the experience before. How many of those scenes have you lived in your life, and especially now that your awareness level is growing so quickly, as awareness levels double each year on the Path of Self Development, as you certainly must be to continue reading this book. Up until now, you've no doubt referred to that situation as *"deja vu."* And, what is that, this thing we so glibly identify with a French term? That reminds me, it was the great Yankees catcher, Yogi Berra, who once said, "that's like *déjà vu* all over again."

You'll find that as you come to grips with the idea of *deja vu* being atavism, (or, perhaps, in some instances, propheticism) that your life will take a stride forward. You will feel much more in control when the condition arises next time. And you will also find that, as you learn the significance of the experiences in yourself or perhaps your patient, your insights will expand dramatically.

When atavistic tendencies begin to occur in us or others, we don't take too much notice of them unless they are either obviously serious aspects of the personality, or they may be pathological... or causes of disease. In which cases, the understanding that we have of the condition can be a most important and valuable source of the healing process.

When we think of man's consciousness as being a Screen of Awareness, we frequently place on the screen elements that are directly associated to the *externa*, or outside influences.

That is, expressions from our own lives taken from circumstances, environment and peers. And, through the build-up of the permanent atoms we can expect that there may well be similar types of experiences that we have had in our past lives. When some of those qualities of the previous lives enter upon the same Screen of Awareness, they will over-lay or over-lap each other and play their part there. So, you may find that you can act out the situation and condition of the past, but put it into today's scenery and today's clothing, furniture, accessories, etc.

For those who are just now becoming aware of the concept of atavism, you may find some difficulty in identifying experiences from a previous life versus those from this life. But, pondering on the conditions as they occur will soon show you the differences.

If the energy behind the atavistic scene is strong enough, then there will be a rush through from your Personal Unconscious. The resultant picture, or behaviour or feeling, may well appear strange and misdirected, because it doesn't seem to fit into the "you" of today.

It is most interesting to see the part atavism plays in the lives of various people whose spiritual development is at different levels of growth. Masters, disciples, probationary disciples, average man and tribal or savage man each have their own series of peculiarities with this concept. Especially savage man, because it is often here where the individual, at this step of the ladder, is extremely susceptible to negative

Tribal Energies. And, with this type of man, atavism can be seen as a tribal entity that over-whelms and over-powers the individual, who is preoccupied and motivated by the force of such a tribal atavism. I'm sure you can think of many, many instances where this behaviour can be seen quite clearly.

But, as we begin the journey along the Path of Enlightenment, atavism is often experienced by us as an expression. This is what Madame Blavatsky was referring to when she said: "The moment you begin to tread the Path, everything that is good in you, and everything that is difficult in you will be thrown to the surface, sooner or later."

AND IT IS THROUGH THE ATAVISTIC MECHANISMS THAT SUCH THINGS ARE, INDEED, THROWN TO THE SURFACE.

It is in the field of sexuality that atavistic existentialism often becomes so obvious and prominent. In psychological terms "existentialism" refers to man's existence on the planet in this life, his situation in the world, his position in the scheme of things, the meaning of his life ... and his freedom to choose for himself his goals and projects, as well as the direction he is taking. It is looking at his need to be responsible for his actions, and his position in life as a result of those actions. It is accepting the results of his decisions and choices that have led him to where he is at this very moment in time. It is the sum total of him as of NOW, and that whatever that total is, it will alter itself by the choices, decisions and experiences that are coming to him ... and that are unique unto him only.

The Buddha's Nose

Existential Psychology is a process of therapy that takes all of the above description into account and uses methods of introspection as the prime therapeutic tool ... not unlike the basic premise behind Psychosynthesis.

A person may have sexual expressions that are bizarre, that are highly unusual, that are perhaps frightening and sickening to most normal people ... normal meaning "generally accepted by the vast majority of the society."

In the animal kingdom, where instinct plays a great part in their lives, we can accept strange sexual behaviour, and are often entertained and amused by some of the antics we see.

The atavism of the particular species speaks clearly through their sometimes extraordinary behaviour, which we call DISPLAY. So, an animal such as a male peacock will inevitably fluff up its feathers into a remarkable display of beauty, intimidation and the promise of power and force. Other animalistic idiosyncrasies incorporate beaks and claws and teeth and sounds and smells ... all of which are expressions of display.

As bizarre and as cute as these things may be to us when we observe them happening, it would do us well to remember which kingdom we have graduated from last and by doing that to accept the fact that we have within us similar display habits that could manifest themselves under certain conditions. The list of such display-type quirks of ours is as long as your arm, but for the sake of brevity, I refer to them as "fetishes."

The Buddha's Nose

What is a fetish? Broadly, I'm talking about any object or body part that arouses the libido or sexual drive that is strong enough to be seen as a pathological condition as measured against the state of normality. This object or bodily part is most usually something that belongs to the opposite sex, although this is not the case with homosexuality.

Often, when the female human sees certain male rear ends, she will perhaps say when asked that she likes his tight little ass. That may well be nothing more than an observation that is connected to the beauty of the male form. On the other hand, if the sight of that tight little ass leads to an over-whelming desire to touch it, to fondle it ... and that desire leads to sexual arousal, then we have a fetish on our hands (you'll pardon the pun).

Or the man develops a fetish for high heel shoes on women. They appeal to him as being awfully sexy (a common fact known to every woman on the planet over the age of three). But, while just observing high heels on a pleasant looking lady may be appealing to him, it is not considered a fetish until he wants to have those heels running up and down his back, which will lead him to orgasm. And, this type of behaviour can easily become the ONLY way he can accomplish orgasm.

That may be regarded by some as being most unusual and strange. But it is certainly nowhere nearly as strange as you might think, as there are literally thousands of such cases reported and confirmed of this fetish alone.

The Buddha's Nose

As you well know, the male has a predilection for the female breast, or the eyes, or the mouth, or the legs or the derriere.

As we continue to observe man and his behaviour, we see that most of those types of stimulations of the female form are "learned behaviours"... our fathers commented on the female anatomy as soon as Mom was out of the room. Our male friends perpetuated the observances as far back in school as we can remember, and George became enthralled with the "male-ism" of it all and became one of the boys by commenting on the looks of the female across the room, as often as possible.

But when that fun time of sexual comment turns into something else...something savage...something totally unpleasant...something driven... something over-powering within the male brain, then we surely are talking about a condition that has ancient lives written all over it. And ancient lives are related to atavism.

Returning to the concept of DISPLAY, what is streaking? It's a form of display. What is so appealing to some couples who feel the urge for sex of some kind or other in what they see as "dangerous" circumstances? Are they hoping deep down to be caught and therefore be able to "display" themselves? And what if only one of the couple is really driven to display, what is the motivation behind the other partner agreeing to the performance? Is that partner expressing a more latent desire for display than the other, or is it the result of a personality that is weak and can't say "no" for fear of losing the relationship? Or, could it be BOTH possibilities?

Perhaps in the weaker partner their Screen of Awareness has been partially usurped by the other partner's strong drive and desire. And the atavistic tendency of the weaker one is merged on to the Screen by the thoughts and energies of the stronger. And before you know it, EACH partner is as deeply engrossed in the performance as the other.

As those of us that are students on the Path know, the last swing around the zodiac, which usually represents our last 20, 30 or 40 lives, is the beginning of the process of what is usually referred to as "tidying up." Getting rid of the loose ends of our nature, as it were, and knowing that we are always concerned about our own atavistic tendencies, because atavism invites our discrimination ... the real from the unreal.

When we understand and appreciate the fact that the soul is without sexual drives, desires or wants, then we must look extremely closely at our own sexual behaviour, and be prepared to view it as an intensely interested observer, keen to isolate and identify the atavistic sexual signs that appear. This includes a close review of asexuality or non-sexuality.

As you begin to get a feel for the potential enormity of the concept of Atavism in your life and the life of others, this introduction to the subject brings with it a lesson of enormous consequences. It is this:

You must now look at and consider the kinds of judgements that you may have toward others.

The Buddha's Nose

You may say to yourself, "Well, I only judge people under certain circumstances. I can go along with this and with that ... but when it comes to THIS in someone else, well that's where I put my foot down. I don't mind some of that, but I can't stand anyone who does this."

That kind of thinking may have been acceptable BEFORE you knew about Atavism...BUT NOT NOW!! Now you can see that for you to make moral or even ethical decisions and judgements about others is entirely unacceptable, and is a clear and definite negative statement about your place in this world, and the state of your awareness process.

People with drug problems, or sexual problems or are suffering from habitual problems that George just won't let go of, you'll see that it will be entirely unreasonable and unwise of you to judge them on various inadequate standards set down by either society, or even worse, by you yourself. Such judgements cannot take into account Atavistic tendencies that they are fighting, or past life expressions that are linked to the atavistic nature within them.

You and I are not going to learn everything we need to know in just this life. No three year old child becomes a 45 year old adult on his fourth birthday. No tomato can ripen any faster than nature allows (even with a blow-torch). There IS no Jack in the Beanstalk ... at least there is no Beanstalk that will grow to THAT size, overnight!

It is NOW that you can begin to consider for yourself your possible Atavistic tendencies. Ponder on what you see, meditate on what you feel and consider what you experience. Each time you do this seriously, and with cathexis, you make

108

a step further up the ladder of enlightenment and the tentative toe on the rung is replaced, firmly, by the entire foot.

As you do this personal introspection, remember that fear is brought about usually as a block that is placed in the way of our growth. Numinousness is a perfect example of that syndrome. There are many times in our lives when we may well show atavistic tendencies. The chief magnet for such tendencies may well be our subconscious mind, a throwback to the past that manipulates our behaviours. This is often childlike in us and is developed in this life through experiences and Authority Figures as well as permeating ourselves with experiences of past lives

"Character, including the aptitude for work, is inheritable like every other faculty." .... Sir Francis Galton.

Among other facets of endeavour Galton was a Geneticist and Hereditarian, as well as the developer of what he called Differential Psychology. He traced and published information on families and their abilities and natural aspects through the use of statistical methods and concepts. He coined the nature/nurture distinction of humanity in about 1883 and considered that humans could be classified according to their natural gifts and behaviours.

His good friend Charles Darwin had proposed that the mechanism of inheritance was what he called 'pangenesis.' This concept considered that 'gemmules' in the bodily fluids were mixed during mating. Galton disproved this theory through experiments on rabbits that showed that blood transfusions would not alter heritable characteristics, although there was still an open question as to the validity of inheritance through other bodily fluids.

He published on a number of related subjects such as:

- Pangenesis;
- Heredity in twins;
- Arithmetic notation of kinship;
- Hereditary deafness;
- Reproductive selection;
- Hereditary colour in horses;
- Racial change;
- Talent and character; and
- Natural gifts.

In his work "Hereditary Genius" Galton presented his concept of 'Eugenics' which was intended to improved and stabilise the human genetic potential. By the time he published *"Eugenics: Its definition, scope and aims,"* in 1904, there was great controversy raging between deep thinkers like H.G. Wells, George Bernard Shaw and Galton himself as to the efficacy of Eugenics.

By 1908 a collection of his articles on Eugenics was published dealing with issues such as:
- The possible improvement of the human breed;
- Studies in national eugenics; and
- Restrictions in marriage.

The Buddha's Nose

Galton assumed that over successive generations, talent and character would find their level based on the degree of intellectual and physical mediocrity that existed in the family. And that a way could be found to manipulate the hereditary process to increase the frequency of desirable human traits over the undesirable, and thereby improve the human condition.

Cesare Lombroso, an Italian physician, psychiatrist and criminologist was very interested in Galton's work on atavism as well as Darwin's ideas of evolution and their relationship to criminal behaviour. He concluded that criminals were actually victims of atavism (what he referred to as 'Atavistic Criminality') and that there were clear indications that future crimes could be prevented through an understanding and acceptance of heredity and atavism.

He also was convinced that social factors played a significant role in criminality, but that at least 40 per cent of crimes were biologically based.

Lombroso's influential work on Criminal Man incorporated issues such as tattooing among criminals and others, (showing the survival of primeval instincts), the primitive characteristics of offspring and the dangerous primeval instincts that could appear where reproduction was unlimited.

His major theory on atavism was that to minimise criminality would require minimum re-productivity, which in turn, would restrict the frequency of socially dangerous primitive instincts, because off-springs of the criminal behaviour tend to exhibit the same highly undesirable social qualities as their ancestors.

It's my experience that well over 80% of our behaviour comes directly though George, our subconscious, and bearing in mind other aspects of behavioural development such as Atavism, it doesn't take long for us to understand the importance of establishing our family history background as extensively as possible. This is one way of appreciating the impact of some of our own peculiar habits, engrams and idiosyncrasies expressed by George, which seem to have no logical explanation to us, and in fact appear completely foreign to our beliefs and general comportment.

If it sounds like I'm trying to sell you something, maybe I am, but I see it as suggesting that you find out for yourself what works, and go for it. Be a super scientist for yourself.

Irving Says

If you wish, make a list of some of the strange behaviours of you and others.....the stranger the better. Then consider each one: does it seem to apply strictly to this world? Is it a family trait? Is it unexplainable? Do you know of anyone in the family with the same habits? Is this particular behaviour completely foreign to the person? Take time to meditate on some or all of these issues and expect an answer.

The Buddha's Nose

Chapter Ten - Kids

"Kids, what's the matter with kids today....
why can't they be more like us,
perfect in every way"...
paraphrasing "My Fair Lady."

This is a particularly tough subject for me to deal with because of the pain that goes with it, but at the same time, there's some really good stuff here too.

I was 27 and about to leave Canada to live in California, when my first kids came along, Scott and Taryn. Their mother, Pat, was the life of the party until it was evident that we had a real problem .... her alcohol addiction and how this changed her pleasant personality into a Jekyll and Hyde. Antabuse served only to increase her hate for all and love for none... the overwhelming physical sickness from the drug reaping days and sometimes weeks of extreme pain, only serving to hate herself and her life even more. Ultimately she died a mean, painful and miserable death from it while I was living in Hong Kong and working deep into the Far East. We had divorced many years prior. She subjected herself to great physical abuse from a series of male creatures not deserving to be called 'men'.... regular assholes of the first water. Much of that despicable behaviour unfortunately came in front of my two kids. Finally, I went for custody of them both, which was granted without challenge or defence.

But the excessive criminal torture (yes, torture) of extreme sexual and physical abuse perpetrated on their mother by her many and varied lecherous male partners, burned brightly in the minds and memories of the kids. To this day we really won't talk about what they went through before I got them away from her, except in the broadest of terms.

Scott certainly never thanked me for releasing him or them from her control, as a matter for fact today, at the age of 55, he has chosen not to speak to me or communicate in any way. Apparently he had decided to blame me for his conflicted feelings towards his mother, and I'm the scapegoat. The last time I saw him was a few years ago at his house and we sat in his indoor sauna in his million dollar plus egotrip and he proposed that we should change our relationship to that of 'friends,' no more father and son. I was the prick of all pricks! I agreed because a small piece of the pie was better than none....right?...wrong! The relationship between us has slipped steadily downhill from there. About a year or so ago Scott's step-son, Sean, age sixteen, died one night under most strange circumstances. There may have been drugs involved, I don't know for sure, because Scott closed the subject to any family discussion.

When Taryn called us to tell us about Sean I phoned Scott immediately and was only able to get a few words out before the tears burst and I was forced to hand the phone over to Toni....I couldn't talk, my pain was so intense. He said he would write me and tell me what happened... haven't heard from him since.

Later, when I share with you my life with my other son, Teddy, I suspect you'll understand why this hit me so damn hard.

As I sit here writing this book I am also considering just what to do about Scott. The pain and disappointment has gone and the realities have appeared. I don't think I want to keep him in my will but I'm struggling with exactly why not. Maybe because the money can go to another source, such as my outstanding daughter Taryn, where only love exists between us. Maybe because I just want to be a horse's ass and punish him for his thoughtlessness. Maybe because my ego is shattered, or my hubris is challenged, or I just simply don't like him anymore, or, or, or .... right now I just don't give a fuck!

I'm sorry about that because Scott's basically a good man, who, I feel, has gotten twisted about some of the more important things in life, like family and responsibility.

But I'm a very, very lucky man...I've found true love twice in my life: once I married it and once I produced it. Toni and Taryn, I mean. I am now learning what it's like to be happily married to an outstanding woman who constantly shares with me what and who she really is. And also what it's like to be the father of a special human being. I am blessed on both counts.

The Buddha's Nose

In her younger years Taryn had more than just a little of the incorrigible behaviour of her father's ilk. She rebelled at her life, the tragedies she saw and experiences she suffered with her mother. The result was rejection of authority in any form. In other words when she was young she was a shitbird. But she came through that period of her life, called me on the mat to discuss and defend my fatherhood of Scott and her, and ultimately decided that I wasn't the bastard that Scott thought I was. But it took some considerable effort on both our parts.

Today, at 54 she is a strong and sincere advocate for the oppressed, sick, old, poor and depressed. She is heavy into community service, loves her work, enjoys one or two Fosters after long work hours, likes to study for degrees and diplomas, loves her cat and her convertible, cares deeply about her family, enjoys snorkelling and cross country skiing and hates it when bad people do bad things...got the picture? Yeah, she's special, mate.

She's also gay and accepts people and their various attitudes to that, but she doesn't flaunt it or defend it....it just is.

Now comes a toughie: introducing Teddy, my third child, from a different mother than Scott and Taryn. His actual name is Edwin Russell Heaton Junior. I don't remember now why it was important to name him after me, I might have been on a heavy duty hubris trip, but there you are.

The Buddha's Nose

He was born with ten of everything required, blonde good looks, smart and happy....but 'different.' I saw that quite early on, probably about three years old....there was something definitely 'different' about him.

One day when he was five or six I arrived home from work and Teddy was playing with friends in the back yard. What I saw and heard was to stay with me until this very moment and probably far beyond. I was in shock! He was playing with six or seven friends, all of whom were girls. He was playing with their dolls and yelling and shrieking just like they were, you know the sound little girls that age make.

I watched and listened as if I was cast in stone, couldn't move. A gay son, holy shit!

The very next day I got the name of the best child psychiatrist in LA, made an appointment for Teddy and me a few days hence, and waited eagerly for the time to come for our visit.

Now, I'm not a real fan of shrinks of any kind as a group. That's because I've had considerable experience with them over the years and found them to be at least as buggered up as their clients, but this guy took the cake. I had just paid him half the national debt for his words of wisdom and this is what he shared with me....

"Mister Heaton, there is nothing at all wrong with Teddy, he's just a normal growing young boy....nothing to be concerned about."

"Are you sure, Doctor?"

"Absolutely"

The Buddha's Nose

I grabbed Teddy and we got out of there pronto. I couldn't get far enough away fast enough from that dipstick.

I was totally convinced from that day on that Teddy was gay, a homosexual, a faggot, an ankle-chaffer, and all those other thoughtless, hurtful, inconsiderate terms that people used then and still do, unfortunately. But, later, I was to find out that I was wrong.

He wasn't gay at all, he was a transgender. He was a female in a male's body. When that became abundantly clear to me I set about finding out all I could about transgenderism. It took me into another world completely.

Teddy's not with us anymore. He either suicided or overdosed, the authorities were never able to convince themselves which was the case. Of course, I don't know either. But I do know that Teddy tried five times to kill himself before the final day, because the pain was too intense.

By the time he died, Teddy was no more and had been replaced by Joan, (named after his heroine Joan of Arc) and he lived in female clothing. He was extremely artistic and esoteric with a great sense of humour and love for others. I miss him every day and see him in front of me right now.

The last time I saw Teddy was in Vegas where Toni and I had gone to meet Joan. She and I went down to the bar for a drink and a chat. The boozing, lecherous men in the room thought they were ogling a six foot gorgeous chorus girl or something. Little did they know.

The Buddha's Nose

Stepkids

I have been stepfather to five kids (four girls and one boy) during my life, so I can talk about the subject with some kind of authority, or at least I think I can. If you can imagine Adolph Hitler having a sexually gratifying life with Sister Theresa, then you can imagine roughly what the tenseness is like that is often created between the parents of a child and a stepchild. Yes, some people can merge their off-springs into a stepfamily relationship with little or no trouble or inconvenience that's all lovey-dovey, or so I've been told. But, don't eat that Elmer, there's a hair in it!

I have found that the age of the kids doesn't matter as the problems are exactly the same. I have also found that my age doesn't matter either because my problems are also exactly the same.

The best tip to tranquillity that I can muster is that both parents become as honest and forthright as possible under the circumstances and treat each other with love, honesty and respect and give the kids as much space as is available. And another tip: try hard to *not* marry someone who already has kids: your own will be hard enough to rear. And one more: be sure to get marriage counselling first thing, as soon as the stepfamily becomes obvious....but not with a shrink, use someone who's been there and has apparently solved the myriad problems themselves.

Someone once said that children are hostages to fortune. I get it.

The Buddha's Nose

I tell you there's a wall ten feet thick and ten miles high between parent and child....George Bernard Shaw

Irving Says

I think this chapter speaks for itself, and anything I needed to say I already have. The important tips and philosophies are contained in the chapter itself....that's all I have to say about that.

The Buddha's Nose

Chapter Eleven - Marriage

When I married Vi I was a tender 20 years old and she was 27. When I married Toni I was almost 70 and she was 26 years younger. In between those two, I had four more wives. Yes, six marriages in all, which means I either know one hell of a lot on the subject, or SFA. I may not be a Mickey Rooney or Elizabeth Taylor, but I think my experience warrants me expressing myself on this somewhat delicate issue. You be the judge and I'll accept your verdict.

Including those six marriages I had a total of nine engagements. The financial cost was: nine engagement rings, cars, houses, jewellery, silverware, libraries, furniture, a lot more money and my reputation. But all that was minimal when compared with the price I suffered on others, kids in extremely unhealthy dysfunctional living conditions with mentally sick mothers (I say 'mothers' because there was more than one of those), my money problems attempting to provide reasonable child support and alimony, with the numbers ever-increasing as one marriage compounded on the next. Before long I was working just to pay for my transgressions, bad choices and improper decisions. Fast Eddie used to say to anyone who would listen that, "A stiff prick has no conscience." Of the half dozen, my third was the only one that I consider to be a total and complete mistake. I knew, well in advance of our wedding, that this was not for me....the problems were right in front of my chipped nose, but I did it anyway. I won't go into detail about that.

At my age now, and with the great power of retrospect, I can see some of what I did in those days to bugger up my life, and that of others too. I realise that I'm lucky to be alive at all, given the mafiosa gang in Canada, husbands and ex husbands that surrounded me and threatened to take me out.....I was either plain stupid, insensitive or bullet proof. When I look back at my track record with women I see something loud and clear....I had to be a rescuer and saviour, which was my main thrust: bringing fair damsels away from their lives of insecurity into the real world....mine. You know what? I think I actually believed that. The fact that I was principally responsible in my mind for fucking them up to a fair-thee-well, in short order, never occurred to me.

Besides being a rescuer of women I was also a fierce competitor...I hated to lose. Winning was the answer to it all.

Now brother, what I'm about to say here is not ego driven but is presented purely as a matter of fact. I'm defending nothing, just explaining something that might help someone. Over my life many women have been attracted to me. I have a good sense of humour, am reasonably good looking, was always perceived as successful in my business, travelled around the world, was a good educator and student of human behaviour and played the piano...and that's the *coup de grace*. To them that explains a sensitivity to life that many men don't have or aren't able to show to women. The piano has acted like a chick magnet more than once: it increased my normal charisma four-fold at least. That made saving those women, who perhaps wanted saving, almost convenient and easy. That wasn't a plan in the front of my brain, but it was a direction that George took on an almost regular basis, in the earlier years especially...the competitive engram was fully formed and vibrating at a young age.

Today, my marriage to Toni is about as good as one can get. I figure I've earned it and so has she. We love each other, and we have found out that communicating clearly with each other is at the very hub of the wheel of relationship satisfaction. At this age she has all the talent and makes most of the money and I'm just along for the pleasure of the trip...it's most enjoyable; for me it's called 'retirement.' For her it's called *stillbustinerassment*.

These days we're into studying Tantra together with outstanding results. We are learning more about being intimate and in the moment. I recommend it without reservation to anyone working seriously to improve themselves... especially Leora Lightwoman's book: *"Tantra, The Path to Blissful Sex."*

The Buddha's Nose

Irving Says

Consider each of the following columns and what they mean to you, and what you think your partner thinks about all of this. A meeting with her/him on this subject is guaranteed to be lively and meaningful to both parties:

The Requirements a Man has of a Woman	The Requirements a Woman has of a Man
Perfection	Wholeness
Nurturing	Cooperation
Respect	Respect
Freedom	Freedom
Acceptance	Acceptance
Validation	Validation
Honesty	Honesty
Responsiveness	Responsiveness
Adultness	Adultness
Recognition	Recognition
Equality	Equality
Friendship	Friendship
Needs Met	Needs Met
Coping Skills	Coping Skills
Communication Skills	Communication Skills
Protection	Protection

You can see from this where the differences between the two genders reside. Men need to study this list carefully and understand the ramifications of each of the items... They are the result of my own personal research on the subject over the years as a psychologist, psychotherapist and full time student of human behaviour.

To assist in better understanding and appreciating each other, or just yourself for that matter, consider the following:

As far back as 1906, an Italian economist, Vilfredo Pareto, created a mathematical formula that became known as The Eighty/Twenty Rule. As far as I can see it applies today as well as when it was first introduced. It stipulates many things, such as:

20% of the people own 80% of the wealth;

80% of the total gross sales of a company come from just 20% of their customers;

80% of a bank's total deposits come from 20% of its customers;

80% of what we wear comes from 20% of our wardrobe;

................and so on

But here's a corker:

My experience shows that 80% of a couple's relationship problems will usually come from just 20% of their known issues...........do you get the point?

Commitment is intended to be a **deal-maker** between two people, but under the surface, out of sight and sound, usually reside some **deal-breakers**. And if there really are deal-breakers then what the hell is the value of commitment in the first place? You can expect a list of 'breakers' to

probably come out of the 20% of issues as suggested above. In an honest discussion between you, what are they and are they real? And don't spare the horses; after all there's an ancient Latin Proverb that states: **necessitas non habet legem----necessity knows no law.**

Chapter Twelve - The Seven Major Fears

My experience tells me that the vast majority of the people I have known carry with them seven major fears. I have a real problem with those so-called pontiffs who talk about 'most people' or 'the majority of people' without qualifying what they're proposing, because they're talking crap in my estimation and I won't listen to that nonsense: it's just a copout! Although they shouldn't, these same screwballs usually make their decisions on published limited statistics that they twist to their own means and satisfaction: it was Henry Clay who stated long ago that 'statistics are no substitute for judgement.' Amen brother Hank.

Quantum Physics has discovered (c 1990) that the OBSERVER influences that which is being OBSERVED. Therefore, this puts fully paid to the theory that one can actually be a *fully detached observer*, because THE EXPERIMENTER INFLUENCES THE EXPERIMENT.

The Fears

- Falling;
- Sound;
- Death;

- Pain;
- Rejection;
- Change; and
- Success.

Some of these are atavistic, some are created in the womb, some are learned processes, some are immediate past life stuff....that is my belief and I'm stickin' to it!

And speaking of fears, I suspect that Mobile telephones will soon affect our brains and make zombies of us, if they haven't already

Irving Says

If you wish, take some time to consider these fears in your own life and that of your partner or partners. Wherever possible, talk about this freely and honestly. This freedom should bring about some definite answers for you to dig deeply into. In this case don't fear change, just go with it. After all, it's one of the very few definites in life; even taxes can be avoided, but change....hmmm, maybe, maybe not.

Chapter Thirteen - Victim

Through my life I have become Victim, Victimizer and Willing Victim many times over. In other words I have been the target of bullies, I have done the bullying and I have allowed myself to be bullied. But why? What affect has all of this had on my life as it stands today? How deeply does this 'Victim Complex' direct my behaviours and relationships with myself and others?

The answers lie within. To bring them to the surface I have prepared a questionnaire to complete, preferably in one sitting you will see the handiwork of Irving behind it all and you will have taken another few steps along 'The Path.'

Good luck!

A VICTIM IS:

A living person sacrificed in performance of a religious ceremony;

a person who has been injured or destroyed by someone else;

a person who has been duped;

a person who has been "walked-over" by others;

a person who has been preyed upon by others;

a person who is or has been attacked by others; or

a person who is unjustly treated.

Circle ALL the ones that have applied to YOU over time:

Sacrificed   a scapegoat   fooled   duped   a pigeon
        a mark

preyed upon   the quarry   swindled   deceived
exploited

used   framed   harmed   hurt   injured
unjustly treated

A **Victimizer** is someone who does the above to another person, or animal, (sometimes even to themselves such as a suicider) I think ***Bully*** is the best description of this type of individual but the person could also be a typical 'poor me-er', but it could be someone who needs self punishment in order to solve their immediate dilemma

A **Willing Victim** is someone who is aware of what is happening, or is about to happen to them, but for a number of reasons allows it to occur anyway

Subliminal Victimization is an energy created below the level of our consciousness, particularly coming from a Group Unconsciousness that has a habit of becoming real under certain conditions such as attending highly emotional sporting events, certain movies, plays, TV or shopping in crowded malls. Any one or more of these can produce spiteful dreams or nightmares of great significance where we struggle all night with the beast of negativity.

Psychic Victimization can occur more often that we might expect. There are times and conditions when we can be zapped by someone from afar; someone capable of sending negativity to us through the astral waves and wishing us ill. I am not referring here to black magicians but more likely to enemies we have gathered around us over time. This has happened often to us awake or dreaming.

Some "classes" of people that are particularly susceptible to victimization :

children,   the aged,

the physically weak,   the "abnormal",

the sexually different,   the obese,

the thin,   the sick,

the ethnics,   immigrants,

sports stars,   the religionists,

the disabled,   the poor,

the disadvantaged,   the ignorant,

the greedy,

women,   men.

It's also possible for us to 'victimise' ourselves when we are overcome with guilt, shame or displeasure with what we have done or not done. **Self abuse** is not an uncommon occurrence, particularly among young adults, addicts of alcohol and drugs, those going through divorce, job hunters, the seriously ill, and those of us who just don't like ourselves one little bit at the time and suffer from the *'Poor Me'* syndrome. These *'Willing Victims'* may be aware of what is happening to them, or is about to happen to them, but for a number of reasons allow it anyway.

Perhaps the most apparent reason for our Willing Victim mentality is the thought that pesters us often that stipulates we deserve what we get and that negative karma surrounds us to make sure we get paid what is owed to us for our past transgressions. When we take the time and trouble to find the negative engram(s) that support this behaviour, and change our thinking, we can expect to alter our dreamworld substantially. But first we must identify the issue or issues that cause the condition. Many times I have seen the situation where a person is being severely bullied and is well aware of what is happening but decides to do nothing about it because, in their mind, they deserve it. Or fear of retribution overwhelms.

Ponder on this

A Victim can actually become a Slave to the severe Bully. This happens when:

The Buddha's Nose

You are bound to, or threatened into, absolute obedience;

You, in essence, become a human chattel;

You are completely dominated by the influence of a drug supplier;

You surrender yourself to the will of another;

You lose the power of resistance; or

You lose the power and ability to rebel effectively.

Irving Says

Please take the time to work through this little workshop.....I can assure you that if you do you will have some clarity about yourself that may surprise you....just like it did me when I first designed the concept. But be truthful, after all garbage in, garbage out.

Write down three times in your life when you have been the victim

1. ....

2. ....

3. ....

Who was involved?

What specifically happened?

The Buddha's Nose

How long did the victimization last?

How did you act and react during this period of time?

What was the gamut of emotions that you went through DURING?

What was the gamut of emotions you went through AFTER?

How has each experience manifested itself in you even today?

Of the three that you have listed above, which one is the MOST powerful and long-lasting in your memory bank?

Why do you suppose that is?

Write down three times in your life when you have been the victimizer

1..

2.. ....

3. ....

Who was involved?

The Buddha's Nose

What specifically happened?

Why did you choose to be the Victimizer?

What type of satisfaction did it give you?

How did that make you feel at the time?

How did it make you feel in later life?

What comes to mind as being the WORST group victimization you have heard of?

What comes to mind as being the WORST individual victimization you have heard of?

When and how did you first learn to be a Willing Victim?

What's a "subliminal" victimization that has happened to you?

What's a psychic victimization that has happened *to you or by you?*

Now, take some serious time to review what you have written down and consider carefully what seems to be shining through.

Chapter Fourteen - Sexual Abuse

The Story of Abner

Abner was a happy boy frog, he did the right things, was good to his parents, loved his friends and enjoyed life. One day, at a friend's house, he was asked to stay for dinner, so he called his Mom and she said ok, but be home before dark. Ok Mom, I will.

Well, Abner didn't know it, but his friend's Dad was a mean old bugger who didn't like frogs one little bit so, when no one was looking, he boiled a pot to steaming, bubbling hot, picked up Abner by the legs and threw him into the pot when nobody else was looking like I said.

Abner reacted immediately and jumped right out, swearing under his breath. The father said sorry, he must have slipped. Abner knew better.

After dinner the father suggested that the kids take a nice cool bath because it was a really hot day outside and a bath would be just swell. He placed a big pot of cold water on the stove and asked Abner to jump in; seeing that it was cold water, he did. The water felt really great and Abner soon relaxed. But nobody knew that the rotten old man was turning up the heat on the stove slowly and stealthily and before he knew what was happening to him Abner couldn't move, he just couldn't get out of there. He was mesmerized. And he was dying.

Abner finally died in that pot, he was boiled alive. The old man had frog legs for dinner and Abner's folks never saw him again. Abner was a good guy, but he just didn't think things through or fight for his survival. He let others take him. Once bitten, twice shy and all that jazz.

The moral of the story is: If things are too hot, get out of there immediately, and always be suspicious of someone who wants to give you a cold bath on a hot stove.

Seriously, you get the message, don't you?

I wish I had known the Abner story when I was young. Maybe things would have been quite different sexually in my life if I had jumped out of the pot right away......but I didn't! I suffered too much from uncontrollable fears; fears of guilt, fears of mental anguish, fears of death and fears that I should never like it, but sometimes I did. What was happening to me?...and then, oh boy, the GUILT!

Something strange went on in my life up until I was about three years old. I have no memory of those years at all. My folks told me that they hired a German nanny for me named Heidi but they let her go before I was four. I was never able to get a satisfactory reason for why Heidi left, I have wondered ever since..... I feel as though I was born with an unreasonable and peculiar distrust of Germans, especially German women. I've had that feeling for as long as I can remember...even before that. When I used to travel into Germany it was impossible to go more than a mile inside the border before I would get a screeching, palpitating headache. Pulsating pain!

It made no sense to me then, but it does now. I think the condition was psychosomatic and had something important to do with Heidi. I'll never know for sure, but I have strong feelings of sexual happenings in those early years. It fits, as you'll see from the rest of my story.

Four or five years later the folks made an on-going decision to send me down to that mean bastard JW's cottage for the months of July and August each year. They thought it would be healthy for me and I'd have a good time. It didn't take me long to find out that it was to be neither! So, usually Mom would pack me up and drive me three hours to the lake, stay a couple of days and 'see you later.'

JW always came down for his summer holidays at his birthday time in July, stayed for two weeks, bullied everyone there, created all kinds of havoc, orchestrated his own lavish birthday party, threatened neighbours, friends and family and left to the relief of all and sundry.

Next door to JW was Uncle Jack's cottage. Although Jack was JW's son, there was absolutely no comparison between the two men, except that they were both medical doctors, nothing else, believe me. I have loved no man more than Jack.

Now, Jack was married to Edna who was the original Wicked Witch of the Entire Compass, not just the West. She was the female version of J.W....not as big, but just as mean and miserable. She hated the world and everyone in it. She must have married Jack for his money because it sure as hell wasn't for love. She gave him fits 24/7. She was finally responsible for his suicide after the family found out that he had a chick on the side that he loved entirely. Interestingly she was of German descent and her name was Heidi. He was so totally love struck that he actually bought Heidi a house on the same street where he lived with Edna the Witch. You may have heard the expression 'love is blind.' Well, in this case, Jack, like our friend Abner the Frog, sat in that cold water as it warmed up until he couldn't get out of the situation, and his demise became imminent and he wound up a released and happy man with no further future. For Jack there was no heaven, just hell on earth, but maybe he's in heaven now, I hope so.

That first summer Edna's father, whose name escapes me, so let's just call him Asshole, came down for a week or two. That was the beginning of four years of sexual abuse because shortly after he would arrive he would get approval from Edna to take me places because 'he loved kids.' She didn't give a shit, neither did my grandmother, Mabel.

As you read this book you will notice how much emphasis I place on AFs, Authority Figures, and how deeply set engrams from these people can and do become.

As I write this, and in years past, I cannot recall exactly what Asshole did to me but it was extensive and didn't leave much to the imagination. Every so often I will have a sudden flash of being on that hill and can see and feel something playing back to me; an instant video of past experiences. Think of what could have happened to me each year on that rock, with a relentless sun beating down, and fear that knew no bounds and you've probably got it.

When he was younger, Fast Eddie suffered from asthma quite badly and this proved a real problem for him as a sportsman, after all, breathing seemed to be important somehow.

One day, quite by accident, he ran into an old friend, David, who told Dad that he had just developed an inhalation hospital in Toronto where he used a product that he had developed in China. It was dark coloured, thick and extremely smelly...the consistency of Molasses and in its composition included some part or parts of horses. I kid you not! When heated and fanned around a room, it created a force that when breathed in would attack and resolve lung conflicts of all kinds...that was David's guarantee.

Dad tried the process, and it worked for him. From then on he was a devotee of David's. A few years later, when I was about nine, Dad signed me up with David as I was having some troubles breathing properly and they both felt that the treatment would have a beneficial outcome for me..

On a Friday afternoon, after his work, Dad picked me up and drove us over to David's Inhalation Hospital, signed me in and David gave me the rules: I would enter the main inhalation room, about the size of a dance floor with grey walls and ceiling. I would stay in that room from 6pm till 8am the next day when Dad would come to pick me up; Saturday the same routine. No more till the next Friday when the process would begin again. I was assigned a locker outside the room and was told to remove all my clothes and place them in the locker until there was a need for them ....that was ALL the clothes because any clothing that was worn into the room would take on the small of the treatment and would need to be thrown away, as the smell would never leave them.

I was given a reasonably white sheet to cover myself with and taken into the inner sanctum. There was one door leading outside to the locker room and toilets, but inside was the barest of equipment and furniture. All the way around the room, attached to the walls, were benches of a soft type of wood, about three feet wide and three feet off the floor. We were given a large fluffy dirty grey towel to use primarily as a sort of mattress, and an equally unimpressive second hand pillow.

There was little lighting in the place and what there was was of very low wattage. You could see around the room barely but as the night wore on and the juice in the machine increased its presence from the fans that blew it, visibility became less and less. By about midnight it was as if we were in a dense fog. The only noises came from the fans overhead that blew the juice out from various size outlets around the room. Other than that, the sounds emanated from the men in the room...coughing, sneezing, moaning, talking, snoring and puking......lots of puking.

That first night a couple of them came for me in the dark. It was as if they had drawn straws and I was first prize. I avoided them until they gave up. But later, around 3am, one of them, the biggest one, returned and caught me sleeping and, with threats, had his way with me. I know that is just an expression, but in my case it was a fact, that's why I've used it. I remember that well. My sojourns with Asshole were child's play...you'll pardon the pun. This was big time paedophilia and I was trapped, at their mercy. My fear of them was so intense that I thought I was going to faint many times over. Unfortunately, I never did.

From then on, for the next six weeks, Dad picked me up on Friday and returned for me on Sunday morning ...and every single night for all of that time I was their 'prime cut.' I was the youngest, I was the weakest, I was the most susceptible, I was the juiciest, I was the easiest. No one ever defended me, even others in the room who knew what was happening to me did nothing at all. I don't know why, maybe they had been threatened too, or maybe they just didn't give a shit about it all and were too sick to care anyway. The lessons I learned in that awful prison no young boys should ever have been faced with...ever!

The room was filled with sick men, some of whom didn't last the six weeks I was there. Many were old and decrepit, some were lustful, big, hairy creatures with gigantic beer bellies while others were unbelievably skinny with bony eye sockets that stared out at you like death itself. You could make out the sockets, but not the eyes. I still see those sockets sometimes in a dream. Some were nice people but very sick themselves. And, of course there were others who enjoyed the sexual company of their peers, but left me alone, and that went on regularly as well. After a while, in that environment it seemed as though all pretentiousness had been waived and it was simply a question of survival of the fittest. Hmmm, come to think of it, in that horrible room nobody was fit, but you get the picture don't you?

I never breathed a bit of this to David, my dad, mom, brother or anyone else...not even Uncle Jack, no one except for my wonderful wife, Toni....until now. Now you know and by knowing perhaps it will help you to help yourself. That's what I'm trying to do, help myself and you.

David left this planet in the early eighties and I never held any of this against him. I think that had he known he would have been beside himself with grief for those who got hurt. He was a good man. His treatment was good too, many poor souls had excellent results, including Fast Eddie, but I don't think I was one of them...but then how could I have been, given what went on for me in his weekend hell-hole.

To this day sex has been my biggest difficulty, second to none. This writing is already noticeably helping me deal with my shadows or to put it in esoteric parlance, my "Dweller on the Threshold." I suspect you've got one or two yourself.

Like many young men and boys I know I was not unique in dealing with the threats of occasional sexual abuse of one kind or another that came at me from men and women too. But after my experiences with Asshole and the inhalation hospital I knew how to accept or reject sexual advances most of the time. I could spot them coming a country mile away, still can. I did get caught sometimes by transsexuals and nymphomaniacs, but that's another subject altogether.

The Buddha's Nose

We are not permitted to choose the frame of our destiny, but what we put into it is ours......Dag Hammarskold

Irving Says

The Mighty, Mighty Frog

The basic blueprint of life on this planet Earth is the molecule known as deoxyribonucleic, or the DNA. The DNA is found in every living cell...from the leaf of a turnip to the brain of an Einstein.

The DNA in the cell of a starfish, when it is uncoiled from its compacted state within its confines, is one foot long. In a bird, it is two feet long. In a man, three feet. And in a frog, over eight feet.

There is something special about a frog!!

The early Egyptian Christians used the Frog as a special form on their Church lamps. Each lamp that had the frog symbol on it, also had the following words engraved on the side:

"I AM THE RESURRECTION"

Much earlier, the Greek and Egyptian Goddess Hiquet, was represented by the Frog. The Goddess denoted "the beginning of life on this Planet"...the importance of water to man's inner nature, and the dogma of "resurrection, re-birth or to be born again."

Back further still in time, the ancient Hebrew scrolls acknowledge that the Frog represented to them their "Creative God."

The Buddha's Nose

It seems that the Frog, as a symbol in a dream or vision, possesses strong messages for the subject of the dream or vision.

Think about that the next time you want to hook up a live frog as bait on your fishing line.....or scan the menu at that plush French restaurant.... RRRibbit.

Chapter Fifteen - Dreams

Or how to help you learn about yourself when you're out of it at night.

I'm hooked on the overwhelming importance of dreams and the significance they play in our lives. My passion will lead to the publishing of a book on the subject before too long.

Understanding a little about dreaming and its implications can be a great advantage as you search for your authentic self. While the subject is extensive I'm presenting you with some interesting concepts of dreams that have 'healing' qualities about them and will provide opportunities to be used in positive and successful ways. ***Dreams are a primary source in helping us peel away the unknown or misunderstood aspects of who and what we are***. And George is a major player in all of it.

Excess Baggage and Dreams

Energy follows thought, and thoughts are things

What kind of dreaming can be expected when the brain is on overload? Messed up, that's what!

Day residue (Freud's term) dreaming is a result of your mind trying to make sense of the day/s activities, issues and problems. In this case a 'day' may be up to a week. There is a strong concept that has been around for a few years that stipulates that if we hold more than seven major issues in our mind at any one time we are automatically in a position of creating Excess Baggage in our lives. I firmly believe it to be valid, for myself and others.

Excess Baggage (EB), has all kinds of negative connotations attached to it. Lack of self confidence is a major concern when EB hits for long periods of time, causing deep divisions in spiritual awareness, soul activity and karma processing. It can be responsible for psychogenetic disparity in future identification of past lives. It is most important to identify, acknowledge and resolve EB as quickly as possible.

Each time we create a Unit of Energy in our mind, the thought of 'Action!' causes our body to create the energy to do whatever is required. Whenever we continue the thought that says 'I need to do this'...and don't do it, a Cycle of Action, Reaction or Inaction has been developed and we are faced with decisions and choices. If we make a decision to Act and Do, then there will be no Unit of EB produced. But, if we make a choice, knowingly or unknowingly, to be Inactive on an issue and just tuck it away for some other day, then the first Unit of EB has been born.

When more than seven Units of EB are in force at the same time, the brain goes into overload as it tries to deal with the demands of problem solving. High levels of stress, sleeplessness, all bodily function difficulties, eating disorders, shakes, anger, lethargy, family dysfunction, work problems, and relationship difficulties can cause lack of confidence and poor decision making ability. Long term stress is dangerous, negative and unhealthy because we're not built to work well that way.

Unresolved issues can create a cybernetic loop as the mind attempts to solve problems through the day and in our unconsciousness at night our Reticular Activating System gets jumbled up through conflictions. Clarity of thought will suffer during the day, which, in turn, will cause the value of our dreams to diminish dramatically.

Irving Says

If you are brave enough, Using a blank piece of paper, write down all the issues you can think of that are incomplete in your life right now on the left hand side of the page, head the column '**Baggage.**'

Example:

Baggage	Excess Baggage
I should have begun my Christmas Shopping for overseas family last week but didn't (5)	
The car should have had its regular service last month but didn't (2)	
I have an overdue book that I should have taken back to the library but haven't (5)	
I needed to make an appointment with the dentist weeks ago but don't want to (5)	
The gutters in the house need to be cleaned out (3)	
I've wanted to call my good friend Jane just to say hello but I'm I'm too busy (4)	
Get my work place in order	

Now, on the right hand side of the page, head a column **'Excess Baggage'** and transfer to it all of the items on the left hand column that you have rated four or five.

Baggage	Excess Baggage
	I should have begun my Christmas Shopping for overseas family last week but didn't (5)
The car should have had its regular service last month but didn't (2)	I have an overdue book that I should have taken back to the library, but haven't (5)
	I needed to make an appointment with the dentist weeks ago but don't want to (5)
The gutters in the house need to be cleaned out (3)	I've wanted to call my good friend Jane just to say hello but I'm too busy (4)
	Get my work place in order (4)

Once you have seven items in this column, do not transfer any more across from the **'Baggage'** column. Now review the left hand list once more to be sure you have allocated the urgent numbers accurately.

Examples:

Turn the page over and on the left hand side create a column headed **Action List** and transfer your seven (or possibly less, but probably not) items. Next to each one enter a **'Without Fail Strategy'** for **immediate implementation.**

As each of the items is resolved they are removed from the pages altogether. Keep adding to the Baggage list as needed. Remember, never more than seven items of the Action list at once. Transfer to the Excess Baggage list those items that qualify for the higher priority numbers. You will feel a sense of deep satisfaction as you successfully manipulate this program and your dream life will be just one of its benefactors. Watch your Day Residue dreams change in significance. Good luck!

Action List	Without Fail Strategy
Christmas Shopping	Start tonight at 7pm at the Mall
Library	Take the book back tomorrow without fail
Dentist	Make the appointment today
Jane	Call her NOW as soon as I'm finished here
Clean up Work Space	Arrive at work early and get workplace in order

Dreams, Sleep and The Reticular Activating System

Sleep that knits up the ravell'd sleave of care,
The death of each day's life, sore labour's bath,
Balm of hurt minds, great nature's second course,
Chief nourisher in life's feast
Macbeth

The Reticular Activating System is where most dreams seem to begin and end. The RAS is also the area of the brain most responsible for awareness in the individual.

An example of this is the story of the man who decided one day that he was going to take this time in his life to fulfil some of his earlier fantasies. This was possible due to his existing financial position, security in his job and relationships. In other words male menopause was beckoning.

So he decided on a new yellow VW convertible. He'd never owned a convertible before and now he could afford one. And they seemed to be somewhat rare, even unique in his part of the world.

A few days later he had completely changed his mind about the VW, because it seemed there was another yellow convertible VW buzzing down the road everywhere he looked. His RAS was in full force and effect!

Sleep is a bi-product of the RAS which is primarily responsible for our conscious and unconscious states, including sleeping, waking and recognition. Some, many, or all dreams may have their genesis in this ancient area of our brain.

Human sleep and waking are part of a fairly constant cycle known as *a circadian rhythm*. Fatigue appears to be the major cause of sleep although other factors play a part in the process.

Normal sleep is divided into two aspects: non-rapid eye movement sleep (NREM) and rapid eye movement (REM).

NREM sleep consists of four distinct stages (all clearly identifiable through EEG recordings of our brain wave patterns)

STAGE ONE: Alpha. The person relaxes with their eyes closed and fleeting thoughts will probably occur. When awakened from this state the person often will say they had not been asleep.

STAGE TWO: Beta. It is harder to be awaked here. Fragmentary dreams may occur. Eyes may roll from side to side.

The Buddha's Nose

STAGE THREE: Theta. The person is very relaxed and body temperatures begin to fall noticeably. This stage occurs about twenty minutes after falling asleep.

STAGE FOUR: Delta. Deep sleep occurs. Very relaxed. Responds slowly if awakened. Bed-wetting and sleep-walking are usually at this level.

In the usual daily seven to eight hours of sleep (depending upon age and other issues, such as illness and stress), a person moves from stage one to stage four of NREM sleep. After the ascension from stages two to three, REM sleep will begin usually within 50 to 90 minutes. This system continues three to five times through the night and by morning the REM periods will have broadened from five to ten minutes at first, to 50 minutes finally. Because most of our dreaming happens in Delta REM State, the result of the night's activities is that we will have had from 90 to 120 minutes of full-on dreaming.

To maximise our dream potential we must look at all possibilities to improve night time inner communication.

One of the most obvious areas to consider is our sleep habits and sleeping facilities.

I have found that each hour's sleep obtained BEFORE midnight is worth two AFTER midnight. This is due to the fact that prana, or life's force, is more easily and readily absorbed in the early evening hours, with the maximum time for intake and storage being 10pm.

Many of us are aware of how good it feels to climb into a neat, clean, fresh, pleasant-smelling, comfortable bed after a long day's activities. But perhaps we don't present ourselves with that pleasure nearly as often as we could or should. Our Dreamland will gratefully thank us each time we do make an effort to build such a cocoon of personal reward.

When we place our bed in the master bedroom we should be aware of certain pre-requisites for sleep and dream benefits.

Where possible we should place our bed so that the top of the bed is facing north. If facing north is not practical, facing east is the next preference.

Sleeping positions have polarities attached to them:

- Head to the North (positive pole);
- Feet to the South (negative pole);
- Front of the body (positive pole);
- Back of the body (negative pole);
- Right side of the body (positive pole);
- Left side of the body (negative pole);
- Right side of the body (female, yin); and
- Left side of the body (male, yang).

Each beat of the heart produces an electrical current that flows through the body from right to left, therefore the preferred sleeping position is head north, lying on the right side, body slightly curved

It is important to look for two other signs of sleep distortion and/or interruption.

Keep electrical radios, clocks and lamps as far away from your head as possible.

Check outside that the house fuse box is not placed on an outside wall close to your head. If it is, move your bed as far away from that spot in the room as you can.

Remember, the more you can do to maximise your dreamland, the more you will receive the benefits, and this also applies to anyone else in the home with you.

Over the years I have noted the following:

Younger women are twice as likely to suffer from insomnia as men, but insomnia is more equally prevalent in both sexes as they get older, divorced, separated, unemployed, in poor health or have children living at home.

While deeper and more pleasant sleep was the usual for those of both sexes who showed control of their lives and their astral bodies.

Dream Oils... as recommended by Toni

To Enhance dreaming -- Clary sage, Nutmeg, everlasting, patchouli, rose damask.

Hallucinations – eucalyptus, peppermint, lavender, sweet marjoram.

Insomnia – basil, bergamot, coriander, mandarin, May chang, bitter orange, sweet orange, petitgrain, thyme, verbena, yarrow, chamomile (german, roman* and moroccan), lavender*, sweet marjoram, myrtle, juniper*, melissa*, neroli, rock rose, angelica, everlasting, linden blossom, rose damask*, rose moroc*, sandalwood*, spikenard*, vetiver, violet, ylang ylang*

Nightmares – lemon, frankincense

All you need is a couple of drops on a handkerchief, and place under your pillow.

* also enhance meditation

Dream Distortion

There are a number of factors that can and do cause dream distortion, especially where more than one factor is in play at one time.

Dream Distortion is often caused by:

- Alcohol;
- Drugs – both licit and illicit;
- Certain foods (spicy, etc);
- Late heavy meals;
- Red meats;
- Exhaustion;
- Stress;
- Smoking;
- Vrittis (over-activity of thoughts) such as..
  - Worry;
  - Anxiety;
  - Guilt;
  - Shame;
  - Fear;
  - Illness;
  - Pain;
  - Anger;

- Frustration; and
- Deprivation.

Following are some significant dream situations that can be particularly helpful as you consider your dream life.

Hemi-neglectful Dreams

Hemi means half. For example hemi-analgesia is a lack of sensitivity to pain on one side of the body. Hemi-neglectful dream messages can come from either the subconscious or the unconscious states and can mean insensitivity to one side of an outstanding conflict between two people. It is important to identify the cause of an apparent refusal to resolve an issue and to objectively acknowledge the situation as it actually exists at the time.

A hemi-neglectful dream often takes the position of the dreamer seeing pain in someone else's life but failing to accept responsibility for the part the dreamer has taken in the other person's distress. This person can often be the dreamer's spouse, child, parent, sibling or close friend.

The dream could take the view that the pain/distress in someone is not caused or contributed to by the dreamer, when the reality is that the dreamer carries a high level of responsibility towards the predicament.

To neglect to take affirmative action to resolve the issue between the two people involved will tend to create a pressure and strain on the dreamer that can be overcome by positive pro-activity on his or her part.

The Buddha's Nose

Hemi-Neglectful Dreams Workshop

Working with a buddy, find a dream that you can't quite understand. Or feels like something is missing, or you have lost something. Maybe use a recurring dream that has components that don't feel like they fit. Then, between the two of you identify the issue, discuss the resolution and apply it.

Lucid Dreaming

'Lucid like a glow-worm' ....Sir Isaac Newton

The word lucid refers to something that is bright, resplendent and clear.

When it comes to dreams, the word means even more: it implies that the dreamer **knows they are dreaming while the dream is actually happening**. A clear fragment of thought or occasionally, understanding of the dreamers' reckonings - the aa-haa! principle.

This is a form of continuity of consciousness, a condition that more often befalls people who are seriously working on their own personal evolvement by getting to know themselves better and better. Interpretation of one's dreams is a sure way to speed up that process. But it's important to understand the concept of 'interpretation.' Write to me and I'll give you some tips.

Marital Dreaming

Marital dreaming is what often happens between married partners when they appear to share a single dream jointly during the night. This is a form of what is usually referred to as a form of Transference. The closer the couple, the more the transference can be expected.

The phone call between friends that does not surprise and has been almost expected on some level is a form of transference ....energy follows thought and thoughts are things.

There is the force of co-issues between them that lie at the subconscious levels of each partner, where rumination seethes and the energy is transferred.

Female Dreaming

Today the typical female Dreamland varies by age, health, social status, financial status, marital status and family and parental status. Then there is Atavism and the part it plays.

Adult women can tend to dream mostly about emotive issues related to the current experiences of their lives that are prevalent on their subconscious minds at the time. Worry seems to be a dream motivator. This is the case even when women understand logically that over 80% of worries are usually a waste of time and do not come to fruition.

Their dreams, as residue of the day's events, often deal with specific issues such as relationship traumas where they are not comfortable in one or more of seven basic areas of possible dysfunction between themselves and their partners. They are:

Wholeness, Co-operation, Acceptance, Validation, Respect, Freedom and Honesty, but there are others too, ...see page 111

Male Dreaming

The Male Dreamland varies by age and health, as well as social, financial, marital, family and parental status and atavistic tendencies

Fear by itself is a huge dream motivator, while worry is usually much less prevalent than in the female.

Their dreams tend to be much more competitive-based and sports oriented than their female counterpart. The will to succeed and overcome is a major issue. Strength, honour and the warrior syndrome usually play large roles in their subconscious thinking and therefore are often converted to their dreamland for scrutiny and mental and emotional relief. Homosexuality versus heterosexuality can be threads that weave themselves through the male life almost from beginning to end.

Shame and guilt, while areas of dream function, are not generally nearly as strong and long lasting as for the female.

For the adult Male, dysfunction in his relationship with his life partner almost always settles around the areas of sex or money, and will usually draw dreams of confusion, anger, frustration, hurt, fear and madness.

Chapter Sixteen - Intimacy and What's Love Got To Do With It???

Love, Love, Love, that is the soul of genius
Mozart
(I've never been able to completely understand what Mozart meant by this quote, but I like it anyway)

Consider this:

Puppy Love is intended to be a rehearsal for the "real thing" later on. But it can happen at any age. Its purpose seems to be to allow the Astral Body (myriad of emotions) to experience all it can and to respond to those new or unfathomable experiences in a way that recognition will set in for the future ... a form of identification.

A limited number of such experiences are well worth while and become part of the "growing up experience" of life itself.

Each Puppy Love is cyclical ... it begins, it inflames, it cools and it stops.

The necessities of moderation in everything we do starts quite often with our young loves, because it's here that we learn the pleasures and sadness of relations with others on this planet.

The Buddha's Nose

The more Puppy Loves we have, over and above what appears to be "moderation," the more susceptible we become in later life to being directed by our Subconscious instead of our Conscious or Super Conscious Minds.

If we tend to run from one love experience directly to the next one when we're young, we can expect to be orchestrated by our Subconscious in later years ... which will inevitably lead to reproducing our younger days when we're older.

If this happens, we can fully expect to suffer from "disappointments in love" on an almost regular basis. The result of which is our instability in relationships. And the pain and grief that this brings to us and to all of those close to us, as well as the trail of despair that usually is part and parcel of the Subconscious influence in this regard, will be clear to see.

Therefore: we must learn to start our young people out early in their lives understanding the power of the Subconscious and the difficulty and beauty of relationships. ***And the absolute necessity for us to help them identify Puppy Love and its overwhelming forces for what it is ... the school of relationship training.***

It seems to me that many men as a group have a problem with Love. And I suspect that many women might agree with that right up front.

I've learned over the years that to enjoy a secure, vibrant relationship women need, above all else, 'communication' with their man, but what that really means is they need 'talking' with their man, and what that really means is that they need INTIMACY with their man.

And that can be a man's first problem with Love...**intimacy.** Numero uno! Number Two is way down the line.

Just what is INTIMACY anyway? First of all, it must reside on a two way street. Then, all the garbage cans must be placed alongside the road for regular collection and we must wait for the garbage trucks to come by, empty the cans, and then we return them up to the house....ready to fill again----*carpe diem.*

To be intimate is to be honest, sincere, confidential, co-operative, sexual, sensitive, close and communicative. But that is not intended to suggest that only positive things can be intimate. We can be honestly negative, or we can sincerely dislike something or someone. *It's to use one's personal expressiveness to be direct and complete. It's allowing the Authentic Self (THE REAL YOU) permission to be unchained and to come into the now. It's Self Empowerment of the first water.*

Intimacy is NOT:

Intimidation, bullying, kitchen-sinking, hurting, over-powering, one-upmanship, thoughtlessness, frustrating or insensitivity to another.

It is NOT lying or cheating or conning

Intimacy is an art form that the more we practice the better we get.

Intimacy has two principals involved; the Sender and the Receiver. Both share equal responsibility for the level of success that is attained through the process. One without the other will not achieve the perceived goal of a happier, deeper and more meaningful and lasting, growing relationship.

The study of Paraproxemic relationships proposes that there are four distinct Spatial Zones in the Western world. These Zones are identifiable particularly between two people, although they can also be seen usually in crowd positioning.

The Four Measurable and Discrete Spatial Zones are:

4.   Public;
3.   Social;
2.   Personal; and
1.   Intimate.

These zones vary somewhat by sound, smell, charisma, beauty, empirical manifestation, culture, sex, age and upbringing. But the toughest to visit and in which to stay awhile is number one.

At the same time Parasocial relationships are an imaginary, unreal or illusionary relationship between two people. For example, when the hit TV series Friends was on the airwaves many viewers felt that they actually knew the performers on the show. They followed them, their trials and tribulations, with emotional energy, worry and anxiety as they would if the characters where part of their family. They even feel the same with the reruns today, nothing has changed.

The Buddha's Nose

The same sort of phenomenon happens in soap operas. These actors become real in their parts, even to the point where when they are spotted on the street they are more often than not addressed by their character name, not their real name.

Stalkers are usually encased in parasocial relationship binding. Some paedophiles would also be classed in this category.

People who are reclusive and lonely, student-teacher relationships, religious bigots, personal heroes, even spousal interactions can fall within the confines of a parasocial relationship and often a paraproxemic relationship as well. Pets can easily play a part too.

Parasocial relationships are often fraught with danger for both people in marriage or long term relationships. It's not uncommon for us to not see the real person across from us, but instead be blinded by not what we see but instead by what we WANT to see. This type of relationship will usually include one or both parties being restricted in their offering of themselves intimately to the other by limiting the level of paraproxemics between them. In other words, keeping their distance.

Then there are all the aspects of loving love that float unencumbered through the ethers: Love is blind. Rose coloured glasses. Lust oversees all else. Getting away from mother. Being considered by one's peers as 'one of the boys.' To defy one's parents. For financial rewards. To escape. Love heals all wounds. Getting too old. Children. Shedding old baggage. Wanting to be cared for. Loneliness. Prearranged. Poor Me. Need a trophy. Don't give a fuck. Take whatever I can get. Free sex on demand. Chief cook and bottle-washer......all just for the sake of loving love! Can you relate?

There are many underlying reasons for why we make arrangements to enter into relationships. Naturally the "in-loveness" syndrome is the most common and the most powerful. But if we don't take adequate time to see each other clearly we are in great jeopardy of failing each other. This will tend to happen where we have a misconception and misunderstanding of each other. One of the most predominate causes of this situation is due to the over-riding effects of unrealistic expectations and opinions that are often the result of strong paraproxemic and parasocial subconscious behaviours *that because of a lack of solid intimacy have not been adequately discussed and resolved.*

It's easier to stay out than to get out....Mark Twain

Irving Says

To establish your current state of intimacy in your life please complete the following questionnaire:

1. **Sexuality**: how do you rate your personal sex intimacy, 1-10

> Giving
> Receiving

2. **Honesty**:   How do you rate your usual level of honesty with most people in your life most of the time? 1-10

How do you rate your usual level of honesty with those you consider are intimate with you? 1-10

What are your feelings about how you have answered these two questions?

_____

_____

3. **Personal Expressiveness**:   how large a part in your life does your level of intimacy play in allowing you to express yourself to others?

Describe in detail, including your feelings on this issue

_____

_____

_____

4. **Communication:**   how do you rate your communication skills with : 1-10

A)   People In General
B)   People At Work
C)   Your Immediate Family
D)   Your Expanded Family

E)   On The Phone Versus Face To Face

5.   Sincerity: When it becomes important to be sincere with someone how does that usually tend to make you feel?

_____

_____

When you know someone is sincere with you how does that tend to make you feel?

_____

_____

6. Co-operation: Do you feel that co-operation is a form of intimacy in your life? If so, why? If not, why not?

_____

_____

_____

7.   Sensitivity: How do you rate your level of sensitivity with most people? 1-10

How do you rate your level of sensitivity with people you feel you are intimate with? 1-10

8. Closeness: Do you tend to feel closest to: 1-10 for each

Spouse, children, parents, friends, workmates

.

Why do you think that is so?

_____

_____

How Would You Rate Your Usual Level Of Closeness To Most People? 1-10

9. **Togetherness**: how do you rate your level of togetherness with yourself? 1-10 for each

    Emotionally?
    Mentally?
    Physically?
    Socially?
    Spiritually?

10. **Authenic Self**: how often would you say you expose the <u>real you</u> to people?

Never   Sometimes   Often   Always

11. **Fear of disclosure**: How do you rate your fear of opening yourself up to others? 1-10 for each

Spouse	children (look at each child separately)
mother	
Father	siblings (look at each sibling separately)
Workmates	friends

12. **Fear of disclosure's consequences**: 1-10 for each

To what degree do you fear the consequences of exposing who you really are ?

Spouse	children (look at each child separately)
mother	
Father	siblings (look at each sibling separately)
Workmates	friends

13. **Parental intimacy**: Generally speaking which parent was/is **most** intimate with you? 1-10 for each

Mother   Father

Generally speaking which parent was/is <u>least</u> intimate with you? 1-10 for each

Mother   Father

14. **Siblings:** name each and rate each 1-10
    Their intimacy to you

    Their intimacy to each other

    Their intimacy to each parent

15. **Victim:** for many of us intimacy was and is a scary
thing. It is something that we feel we must avoid. It is not
comfortable giving or receiving. At a previous time in our
lives those feelings have been generated in us through some
sort of impressive experience. At that point a stimulus and
response mechanism and engram was established that we
still carry with us today. There was a time when we were first
introduced to intimacy and that introduction has permeated
our psyche ever since . It was not a pleasant experience,
quite the opposite.

How old where you the first time you became a victim of
intimacy?

Who was the perpetrator?

Describe the circumstances and your feelings then and
now

_____

_____

_____

_____

16. **Perpetrator**: have you ever knowingly and consciously used intimacy to victimise someone else? If so, who, when, where, why and how?

_____

_____

Describe the circumstances specifically and how you feel now about it

_____

_____

_____

17. **Review:** the previous 16 questions have been structured in such a way as for you to personally attain some knowledge about your current status regarding intimacy. Please carefully review the questions and your answers and as you do so make any changes you feel are necessary, bearing in mind that usually the first answer we give is the right one.

The Buddha's Nose

What appear to be the major issues for you as you review your work?

Who are the people that seem to play the largest role in your current appraisal of your level of intimacy?

What are the most significant things you are beginning to see about your life and the life of others around you?

As you begin to see the obvious patterns that will become apparent, write them down on a separate piece of paper for your consideration later.

Finally, write George a letter outlining steps that need to be taken to improve your current intimacy levels with others and end the letter with the creation of an appropriate affirmation to begin the change command.

Chapter Seventeen - Walk The Talk And Talk The Walk (Yes, That's What I Mean)

Of course we don't just communicate through our various levels of intimacy, but HOW we communicate those needs, wants and feelings is an issue as well. One of the best, and yet perhaps the most difficult, is through the process we call 'talking.' Many men are almost as threatened by just 'talking' to their partner as any other form of communication they may employ....and intimacy, forget it. Sometimes chocolate and/or flowers is a form of 'talking', so is going out for a nice dinner, a drive in the country, washing the dishes or taking pressure off some other way. Often that form of 'talking' is called 'fore play.' Strange isn't it? When a golfer yells "fore" he is warning someone that there could be trouble ahead. Hmm, now back to 'fore play.' Just kidding!

There are a number of forms of 'talking' that have been automatically set up within us through a background of established engrams, coming from Authority Figures, that have influenced the way we present ourselves and 'talk'....our parents are a prime example and can often clearly be seen as such when we, quite by chance, hear ourselves mimic their method of 'talking' using their same words, tones, inflections and sometimes even their inverted logic. Yuk!

The Buddha's Nose

I believe that good 'talking' is good conversation and good conversation is good art, therefore there is an Art of Conversation available to all of us.

My experience says that by and large we are patternistic creatures, creatures of habit, that have a tendency to form 'talking' patterns when we're young, and stand by them, until we are made aware that there is a better and more successful way to communicate. I'm not saying this fits 'all people' or 'most people' because I haven't met all people or most people on the planet, but I've met my share and that's my experience after lo these many years.

'Talking' that is purposeful and elegant should be viewed as a Therapeutic Tool because it affects the human aura by expelling old energy and replacing that with new mental, emotional, physical and spiritual forces within.

The Art of Conversation should be taught as a 'must' for any Counselling Course ... and in all High Schools

How do you relate to the following forms of 'talking'?

* INFORM-TALK: Refers mostly to objects, the environment, the past, present and future or part of a learning process when used to stimulate the inquisitive mind and when expressed clearly can be useful and interesting. But when NOT expressed interestingly will tend to be boring and often ego-based.

* DATA-TALK: Typically a male-oriented form of communication used between men intending to infer a closeness or bonding between them that is often "sports-

driven" and is related to the "beast-of-the-jungle" attitude. Usually highly left-brain oriented.

* MOOD-TALK: Emotionally based (hurt, anger, love, frustration, anxiety). Often verbalizes an area of communication already taken care of, and is used as a release and review. Depending on its use, it can provide the accent (either subtle or sensitive) for Mood-Signalling.

* ASTRAL-TALK: Usually the domain of the female, and is particularly prevalent when "the girls" get together. It is built around emotions, feelings, sensitivities and desires and serves as a release from what is often seen to be the male-domination society.

* EXPLORE-TALK: Considers and expresses opinions. Often takes the form of Play-talk which signals an opening of the "ear-waves" for fun and lightness. Can be aesthetic, such as talk about things creative, beautiful, poetry, painting, music, art...and is used as "soul-release."

* SOUL-TALK: The ability to express one's self on the deepest possible level of spiritual congruency and when the small ego becomes the large Ego, or soul, when Unconditional Love is expressed and exudes. These are the times when BOTH parties are brilliantly aware of each other's immortality.

The Buddha's Nose

* GROOM-TALK: Also known as "small-talk" and is of little real value, UNLESS the individual using it is either Expressive or Amiable (particularly Amiable) where it is intended to settle the speaker into the scene much more so than the listener. It is usually polite, social chatter that serves to maintain social togetherness.

* HIDDEN AGENDA-TALK: One form of talking that is not easily spotted at first because it can appear to be another form altogether. This requires the listener to be particularly attentive to the speaker's words and actions, and to look for the first signals that show themselves as to the REAL purpose for the talk. One classic signal is that the subject matter under discussion is quickly and succinctly switched in its direction and content, although that will often happen cautiously and not blatantly.

* SELF-TALK: Something of which we should all do a great deal more than is usually our way. This is the time to ask questions and send statements and messages to the Super-Conscious and/or the Subconscious. It is important to be aware of the fact that Self-Talk happens when DIRECTED FROM those two levels, as well as when we direct it from the Conscious level. When the Self-Talk is DIRECTED from either the Super-Conscious or Subconscious levels, we call it INTUITION.

* BODY-TALK: Non-verbal expression. The use of the body to send signals and messages often as "boosters" to

other forms of talking but also works as a strong indication of the Subconscious line of thinking that may be present. As we learn the techniques of responding consciously to the other person's subconscious actions, we begin to establish rapport by "harmonising" at the lower level.

 * POOR ME-TALK: This is a "dumping process" that occurs usually with those people who are emotionally weak or overly distraught and is used by them to play on the listener's sense of sympathy; which they hope will lead to an acceptance by the listener of their condition; which when accomplished, will lead the speaker to an inner feeling that they can use their predicament as a valuable and successful lever resulting in obtaining what they desire. This is particularly easy to spot when the "Poor-Me" attitudes are not directly related to the issue under discussion.

 * CREATIVE-TALK: Highly indicative of an active and mobile right-brain process. It includes such things as effectively using the imagination; painting vibrant word-pictures; developing and expressing new lines of thinking clearly; using newly-coined words, sentences or expressions. The home of Neuroplasticity. This can often be spotted as a clear and precise creative sign coming from the Super-Conscious.

 * NO TALKEES-TALK: The Silent Treatment, a real killer of relationship happiness because it brings with it great big bully factors. It's also completely disrespectful of the

person that receives it. Usually it accompanies gobs of anger that have been refused direct exposure to the world and harbours within itself as a complete scene...silence, facial expression of that anger, fear to others and righteousness.

* KITCHEN SINKING-TALK: Men tend to use it as a defence mechanism and women tend to use it as an attack vehicle. Big league kitchen sinkers are experts at changing subjects around to their way of thinking and can often get their opponent so confused that they have nowhere to go...except home or to bed, alone!

Irving Says

Talking is a form of communicating that has obviously great value attached to it....providing the person being talked to not only 'hears' but 'listens' too, and that's the rub, LISTENING . Too often when someone is talking to us we have a tendency to start preparing our response to what's being said instead of just listening and then responding. The difference is dramatic.

Toni and I understood years ago that many of our students weren't really **listening** to what was being said to them, they were just **hearing** words; their emotive right brain was already busy building a case of response to part of what they were hearing rather than dealing 100% with what was being presented by the talker. This often led to out of control emotions when what was really important and necessary was good old fashioned left brain logic.

So we devised a plan. It seemed crazy at first but it worked a treat.

We had the students form couples and sit facing each other and we made student A the talker and student B the listener. Student A was given a five minute scenario to talk to B about and B was instructed to interrupt at any time he/she had a question or a comment to make. Then the situation was reversed and B was given the five minute scenario with A instructed to interrupt or comment anytime. Finally, both A and B discussed their experiences in detail and it soon became quite evident that there was a lot more 'hearing' and a lot less 'listening' than there should have been.

Next a scene was created where A would place his/her two thumbs in each ear and wiggle the hands. For this signal B would stop everything, sit down quietly and easily and listen, because A was about to tell B his/her truth and B would listen with his/her ears, eyes, feelings and complete focus....no interruptions, no bodily expressions, just complete focus on what was being presented. The scene was to take no longer than five minutes and no less than four. Then A would sit quietly and listen to B responding quietly and matter-of-factly. Then both parties would discuss their outcomes and feelings regarding the new communicating technique. The results were extremely positive.

The students were advised that the 'thumbs' technique was to be used only under certain strong conditions were communication was suffering and anger and arrogance were showing through instead of resolution. They were told that both parties must understand the importance of the system

The Buddha's Nose

and that when it was called for by either party the other partner would cease whatever he/she was doing immediately and sit down ready to receive the other persons' truth, honesty and sincerity without fear or trepidation. And the responder would receive the same fair and equitable treatment and understanding as the presenter. It was recommended that five minutes each way was more than sufficient time.

Once both parties are comfortable with the concept the results will definitely speak for themselves. Enjoy!

Chapter Eighteen - The Big D

I hold that when a person dies
His soul returns again to earth
Arrayed in some new flesh disguise,
Another mother gives him birth
With sturdier limbs and brighter brain
The old soul takes the road again

An excerpt from John Masefield's poem "A Creed."

By now you are probably aware that I had more than my share of death threats, experienced the light at the end of the tunnel enough times to know that it well and truly exists, faced death-defying physical predicaments, sickness and otherwise ...and that has made me think about an interesting subject: death itself.

And speaking of death, here are three important words:

Thanatos

Human death may often be instinctual but is always a complex universal drive known as **thanatos**. At some stage we all know it's coming... death, that is, but we don't know when because it's a manvantara or full circle, like the daily appearance of the sun or moon, like a good night's sleep, like marriage, like divorce...or like reincarnation

The Buddha's Nose

Schadenfreude

Sometimes when we hear about the death of bad people like Hitler or Stalin, or murderers and rapists, we find ourselves filled with almost pure joy because their demise fills us with a strange pleasure created from their atrocities being called to ultimately answer for...and that makes us feel good...***schadenfreude***....we probably shouldn't feel like that, but we do and so what?

Omnishambles

By some of our standards these bad people are omnishambles, meaning totally and completely fucked up. But even so, sometimes death is perceived to be too good, too soon or too easy for them and we may feel jilted, which could lead to us feeling a little bit ***omnishambles*** ourselves

But death is a natural process, a punishment, a relief or a shock. It is karmic in its conclusion and dharmic in its infusion.

Is it the beginning and the end, or is it the end and the beginning?

How will we know, and who will we tell?

Death is a gamble. Not that it's coming or not, but when and how. Do we really come into this world alone and leave the same way. Is it that simple and yet that complex?

Irving Says

Before death gets here we need to do what we can to prepare for the inevitable. One way to do that is to 'clean out the cupboard' of shit, mistakes, problems that we've caused, hurts we have been responsible for, the blame of pain we've placed on other's lives and futures, and the list of betrayals we have imposed on others ....especially women.

How do we do that? We use some or all of the techniques and philosophies expressed in this book as a way to help us become authentic, to get rid of the personal garbage. When we have reached that position, we can do no more. But mate, I suggest that you get started right now...nothing ventured you know. And I'm right there with you myself!

Chapter Nineteen - Stubby McNames and Uncle Jack

Stubby McNames and Dad were friends and neighbours two streets apart who enjoyed sharing time together at the Club usually on Fridays after work to avoid the traffic, at least that was the line they tried to sell their respective wives, who never really believed it, but so what? Dad in the Insurance business and Stubby in Stocks and Bonds meant that they both had their offices in the same financial building in downtown Toronto so they would touch base a few times during the week just by chance. But the Club on Friday was NEVER just by chance, it was ritual... just a couple and then on home.

One day, over his first Scotch and water, Dad shared a slight family problem he had on his mind with Stubby who by virtue of his profession, was a great listener and thinker....after all, thinking and listening sold war bonds didn't it? He explained it this way: my Mom (Short) had started to take a serious interest in my fiddling around on the family upright piano where I was making music through a slight talent in being able to play by ear. Her original urge to impress me with knowledge of the muse began with her convincing me to take classical piano lessons with Mrs Steinhauser who came with the credentials that had appealed to mom's soul apparently because before I knew it I was in Mrs Steinhauser's home, sitting at her Baby Grand being tutored. (***I now digress for a few moments from Dad and Stubby's conversation,***

My first lesson of an hour was ok...boring as hell but ok, learning to play the scales but for the next seven days it was pure hell scales, scales, scales. Then came the second lesson a week later when I found out who Mrs Steinhauser really was. She was a German Jewish Nazi sympathiser, she was a Major General in the SS corps, she was Hitler's mother twice removed, she was the Commandant at Auschwitz all rolled into one mean bitch of a monster who carried a three foot ruler under her left arm and when I goofed, which was often and regular, she attacked. Before long my knuckles were purple and so was my rage. I lasted two more lessons and that was that. My parents were disappointed. I went back to picking out chords and melody again, as soon as my hands had healed (that's a little poetic license there, but you get my point)

Back to the Club

As Dad told Stubby his tale he was vaguely aware that he had heard somewhere that Stubby played some piano himself although he had never heard him actually play, even though the two had been to each other's home a number of times.

Stubby was a good listener, remember? And out of that ability came a serious part of my future which to this day I thank him profoundly for what he gave me that very evening.

The Buddha's Nose

"Eddie, listen my youngest son, Paul. He has been playing the piano by ear for a few years now and I've been coaching him myself and if I do say so he's pretty good. Why don't I bring him over on the weekend to meet Ted? The boys don't really know each other because they go to different schools and have different friends but I think they'll click."

Stubby didn't know it but by then I had been out of school for three years and was sixteen, the same age as Paul.

Saturday afternoon came and with it the McNames Duo. Without further ado Stubby sat down at our upright like he had just paid the last instalment and now owned it outright, played and sang *"Ain't She Sweet"* with joyous gusto, I mean he brought the whole house alive in seconds. Then he had Paul play the same song with the same chords and I was mesmerised, so were my parents. From that day on two things of great significance began in my life and the life of my family. And, oh yes, I learned to play *"Ain't She Sweet"* too, still do.

One, Paul and I became a partnership and created the name The Four Hands. We played together on one piano at the Yacht and Golf Clubs in town, the YWCA, Saturday night dances as the intermission talent and other similar gigs. On Friday nights we played for the Young Women's Christian Association where men and boys were not allowed to even enter the building.....my, my, my!

And, Two: Stubby was an impressive man, well over six feet and 250 pounds, short on hair, long on smiles and loved people. He liked our piano and the fact that the two boys were doing so well that he decided to come over more often. And he sure did. But HOW he did it is the corker. It could be any day, after work, during the weekend, anytime, if our front door was unlocked in he would come unannounced, head straight for the upright and off he'd go.... *Five Foot Two," "Cecelia," "Louise," "Shine on Harvest Moon," "Walkin' My Baby Back Home,"* etc. He'd play maybe three songs, sing them at the top of his voice and leave, no goodbye, no wind your watch or kiss my ass, just gone till the next time whenever that might be. I loved him and still think of him endearingly. Even after I had padded the piano in studded red leather, well vinyl leather anyway, with a mirror across the entire keyboard backing he still came, maybe out of curiosity as to how I was able to still be alive doing what I did. It actually looked pretty good and the folks got over the shock in a few weeks after they came back from one of their annual holidays in Florida.

The Four Hands got better and better and finally mom's friend who was a pianist for the Boston Symphony, Ming, remember? asked us if we would like to practice at her home on her two Baby Grands. We did a few times but finally we decided we were meant to use just the one piano for the two us. Finally, the world took each of us into its awaiting breast and we went our separate ways towards more of life's challenges. That portion of my life an extremely enjoyable experience.

Why do I tell you all of this you might wonder. Well, as I ramble through my life brother, whatever be my goal, I've

The Buddha's Nose

learned to keep my eye upon the donut, and not upon the hole. Experiences we have along the way often highlight our behaviour, our goals, our expectations, our needs and wants. Reflecting on these positive experiences causes within us a jolt of pleasure and fond remembering of times gone by that are strong friends within us for ever, and all we need to do to enjoy them is to bring them back to our consciousness.

Here's another one.

You know how much I loved Uncle Jack and the great times we had together. Well this one is 'Stubby-like' in nature but you'll see my point.

Many years when it was time for me to go to Grandad's cottage for the summer it was the same time that Jack was taking his two weeks' vacation and I would drive up with him in his smart, black (all cars were black in those days) Ford Coupe, just the two us as his family usually came a few days later. We developed two rituals that stayed with us as long as we were able to take that drive together.

The first one was marvellous; it began when we turned off the main highway on to the washboard gravel road of about twelve miles that led to the cottage. The narrow road was always bumpy but besides that it was hills and vales, hills and vales all the way...up and down. Jack became an expert at knowing exactly when to gun the car as he approached the hill and then when to take his foot off the accelerator at the very top so that as we dropped down the other side our stomach went with us slightly later. Ten or twelve miles of sheer ecstasy.

The Buddha's Nose

When we arrived at the cottage it was very early summer and the temperature was still quite cool. The first job was to open up the building to air it out. The second job was to check that the two western saddles were okay and had survived the elements and were ready for the race. The saddles were placed side by side on the floor of the main room of the cottage which was about thirty feet long, beside the Victrola that played cylinders, that's right cylinders maybe about eight inches long and two inches wide, like an extremely healthy hot dog, that sound emanated from when a needle scratched the surface as it spun around....long before records.

The Old Vic Blared. The race began. The winner was the one who 'rode' to the other side first. You sat on the saddle, grabbed the horn at the front and scooted and skidded your way along the floor by digging in your heels. There was great whooping and screaming and the music was blaring and the floor was creaking and the fun was momentous. Amazingly I won most of those races year after year. Jack must have been getting old I guess, can't think of what else it could have been. The Fat Lady sang way too soon!

Stubby and Uncle Jack are memories of mine that defy time and space. They are often my protectors against the world and its insanities. I can't recommend highly enough that you use some of your own fond memories of love and excitement when you are in need of some TLC, or use mine if you like. It is great, great medicine!

The Buddha's Nose

Irving Says

Abraham Maslow was a very successful psychologist who had a different slant on things human. Instead of doing what most other compatriots of his did he decided to find out all he could about 'well' humans, what made them happy and healthy and well adjusted and when he found out he published what has become known as Maslow's Triangle. It shows how he saw humans developing, growing, maturing and using their lives in positive ways. He believed in the idea of people using their past positive experiences in life to nurture them whenever they needed that the most.

I'm proposing the same thing. Help yourself to the fruits of your labours. Use your positive life experiences whenever you can. They're there for the taking, so take already!

The Buddha's Nose

Chapter Twenty - Years of Pain

When I was about eighteen, my baseball team had just won our league championship and had agreed to play a series of exhibition games outside of Toronto and primarily in certain country areas of the Province, against teams of good calibre. Our first series was three games with a team in Hamilton, Ontario over a weekend, Friday night one game and one each on Saturday and Sunday. It was a tight schedule but Hamilton was only an hour or so from Toronto and it all seemed feasible, I guess.

The team bus left at noon Friday, dropped us off at our hotel and then picked us up at six o'clock for the trip to the park and the game under the lights. That worked well for everyone except me as I had to work until about two and then catch the next bus to Hamilton.

I arrived at the terminal with time to spare, no rush. I sauntered up to the ticket window and as I did I happened to notice, sitting demurely on a bench near me, the Vice President of the Blue Rinse Society...maybe the President, maybe even the Chairman of the Bored. She was classic, the granny glasses, the appropriate clothing, the whole bag of tricks. I dropped my travel bag on the floor beside me and turned to the window, where no one seemed to reside. I steeled myself for a reasonable wait for service.

The Buddha's Nose

"My poor darling," she said, cooing in some plaintively undistinguishable foreign accent. The Vice President stood close beside me stretching to her full height of maybe five feet in heels. Her perfume overwhelmed me with distaste.

"Excuse me?"

"Oh, young man, please pardon me but when I saw you here and noticed your face I just **had** to talk to you. How terrible is your acne and how terrible is your life because of it. What has God done to you and for why."

None of these was a question, just pure statements.

"How long has this condition been with you?"

A clerk arrived at the window just at that moment which allowed me to revamp and get away from the creature with no further ado or adont. We won two of the three games by the way.

Another time I was having a shoe shine, which was a habit of mine, and sitting up on the stand while being worked on. A man in his sixties of seventies, white haired, well dressed was walking by and stopped, maybe to line up for a shine himself, but I doubt it. He zeroed in on me almost as if he was in some kind of trance. The he moved to the side of where I was sitting and beckoned me to lean over.

"Listen son, I can see that you have real troubles with your skin but I can help," he confided to me.

"Oh?" I was shocked but I listened

"Yeah, what you need is to change your oil regularly, I mean REGULARLY."

"My oil?"

"Yeah, your oil, your sexual juices, get it?"

194

The Buddha's Nose

"Yes, thank you."

Off he went his good deed done for the day, maybe the week. After that it was as if a magnet of some kind was attached to me and I must have heard that same concept presented to me without my request at least twenty times, maybe much more in retrospect.

I dealt with extreme acne for many years and my face was so bad that I had real problems just looking in the mirror. Today, all of that pain is still deep inside me. I didn't know then and I don't know now how girls and women could have found me attractive but fortunately some did and I'm grateful for that. I know that I'll carry that embarrassment and grief with me forever because even today I strongly resist having any picture taken to the extent that if I must I will make a funny face in the hopes that the picture will never see the light of day. I still remember the times I had to have pictures taken for work for papers or magazines and when I saw the air-brushing that was done I was sick inside just a little more each time.

Irving Says

Sometimes we're hit with beanballs that knock us for a loop or two. And we carry that crap with us day after day hidden below the surface until something happens to bring it up. Like I said before HARDEN UP and look to your positive experiences for salvation. They're there for the taking.

Chapter Twenty-One - The Wolf

A year later we won our league championship again and once more we set sail to the hinterlands to test ourselves against the country boys. This time it was Sudbury, Ontario and we were up against good athletes and a strong hometown atmosphere so we knew we were in for it. It was set for three games over a long four day holiday weekend so early Friday we departed with expectations that we'd wind up home some time late Monday. Most of us did. Some of us didn't.

We were billeted in a lovely area that was usually intended as a holiday camp but closed as it was now late September and available only to us. It was a gem settled in a ravine surrounded by majestic hills. A single track railway line went from town twelve miles away to the camp. It was used in season to send in equipment, supplies, mail and stuff like that there. (I know, I'm just having some fun)

Our hosts had made a couple of small buses available for our use and once we were all happily ensconced we decide to take a drive into town. The town, whose name escapes me now, was a few miles from Sudbury but it had a couple of pubs and some horny women, or so we had been told by the locals. Well, as we found out, the pubs were there, anyway.

The Buddha's Nose

We tied one on okay, don't you ever worry about that. Drunken skunks.

Somehow or other I fell asleep in someone's house in town, on the floor I found out when I awoke. The guys had been searching for me for an hour or more apparently but finally decided that I must have taken a cab back to the camp and left me at 2:00 am.

I staggered to my feet, thanked my drunken host most graciously (whom I don't recall at all now) and left to find a cab. Are you kidding me? A cab at 2:00 am, I don't think so!

By then I was sober enough to realize that my only way home was to follow the train track that ran right through the little town I was in. I was smashed enough, young enough and stupid enough to think that that was a really good idea.... WRONG!

I set out for camp with a fair amount of moonlight, certainly not full moon but enough to see the tracks reasonably well. I knew it was twelve miles...a piece of cake, right? Yeah, right.

I'm not sure when it happened exactly but I think it was about half an hour along the tracks that I got the feeling I wasn't alone. I don't know why, I didn't see or hear anything strange or unusual, but the hairs on the back of my neck were dancing The Tango for some reason. The weather at that time of the day was cool to cold and when it clouded over it was as dark as the inside of a full can of Bundy and Cola, it was as dark as Prince's hairdo, it was dark. But when the clouds parted however briefly and the moonlight shone through I could at least see the tracks under my feet.

The Buddha's Nose

The terrain was "Canada rough" I call it. Trees, big rocks, slight hills on either side of the tracks. The rocks served as chairs for me to sit on when I needed a rest. Each rest saw me more sober than the last one.

I was resting when the truth hit home: I had company, I could feel it now all the time. I was scared shitless and that's an understatement. Then I saw it. Two lights close together across the tracks from where I sat. Then I spotted two more and two more after that. I knew it wasn't my imagination. I stood up slowly, facing the lights across from me just as the moon's flow, just for a moment, expanded. And I saw them then.

It was a pack of wolves, six or eight, fully grown, apparently curious about me because they weren't licking their lips or chomping their chops. But they were one scary sight. I began to walk slowly along my side of the track careful to stay on my territory wondering what do I do now? I had no experience nor had I read anything about a situation like this. Oh, by the way, all at once I was stone cold sober and you could take that to the bank and borrow on it.

About then I saw two empty beer cans on the track. I picked them up for some reason, maybe because I saw them as secret weapons to drive away the panting beasts. When I turned I saw the pack about five yards behind me on the other side cautious and tentative with a leader that seemed to be quite clearly operating in that function. He was a big grey, sturdy and light footed.... and focussed on me entirely.

The Buddha's Nose

Mile after mile went agonizingly by but, surprisingly, we all seemed to be reasonably comfortable with the situation that existed. I started to clash the beer cans together at regular intervals and sing songs as loudly as possible. The first few notes from my mouth should have been enough for them to attack right there. But the sound probably scared them and made their little ears buzz. When I stopped to rest so did they but we each stayed in our own territory. Now THAT was a real territorial imperative. Later, I found out that what I did with the cans and the singing was exactly what I should have done given the situation. They must have enjoyed the entertainment and not thought too much about their stomachs because if they had I wouldn't be writing this epistle, would I?

Finally I reached the last hill and gazed down into the valley and the camp below. Flashlights were coming toward me from some of my team mates who had heard the raucous noise that I was making all along the way and were coming to find out what the hell was happening. The first sun's rays were about to break through when I turned to say goodbye to my furry associates but they weren't there. They had gone when they heard the guys coming towards me I guess. Surprisingly none of my teammates queried the authenticity of my story, probably because they could see the state I was in when I arrived at the camp and accepted the truth I spoke.

That afternoon, still slightly inebriated and/or hung-over to a fare–thee-well, we won our game, but that was the last one we did win that weekend.

The Buddha's Nose

I can now say in retrospect that I wouldn't have missed that night on the tracks for all the beer in Germany but at the time, when I was in the deep cuka, I don't think my feelings were the same as they are now, do you?

The lesson to be learned from this experience is that sometimes life dictates how and where and when we will be tested and how we perform when the pressure is on. It's a barometer of our mental and physical strength and helps us ascertain our level of Authentic Self. We will be presented with certain, unforeseen at the time, tests of our courage and resolve.

Some we will pass and others we won't. But all will be important to our understanding and appreciation of our Authentic Self. Those that you passed take proudly forward into your life for they are badges of strength and power. Those that you didn't aren't lost to you, they are simply things whose times have not yet come and will no doubt be offered again to you later in this life or the next one. Always give great credence to your badges because they are there to serve you well.

The story also suggests the need we seem to share for having in place certain boundaries in our life, like those the wolves and I automatically fell into without any apparent difficulty. But it's not always that easy and sometimes we have to fight for our boundaries and others don't always like that.

So do it anyway, see your boundaries clearly and put them into place. Eventually everyone will thank you for your courage and your maturity. And so will you. Go for it now.

The Buddha's Nose

Irving Says

Who and what is the Wolf?

Milton said that the cry of the wolf was an inarticulate sound. Was he right? Did he mean the actual cry of the sound or was he referring to the other meaning of the word 'cry' when used to describe the wolf. In that sense a 'Cry' of wolves means a group of them or a pack. Shakespeare used the word to describe humans as well when he wrote: 'Would not this get me a fellowship in a cry of players?' Is that where he may have seen the inarticulation?....in the group.

There are many types of wolves most of which can be traced back to the common dog. There are European, American, Tibetan, Indian, Tasmanian wolves as well as the Eskimo dog which is specifically bred from dog and wolf.

"Don't wolf down your food." "Keep the wolf from the door." "He's a wolf in sheep's clothing." "He's a wolf with women." "She cries wolf too much."

Bad imaging!

So is the wolf negative? Yes! But is he also positive? Absolutely! Why is it that so many humans are tied almost inextricably to their pet dog? Is it the wolf within?

"Wolf Man" was the term given to Freud's most famous patient. The man was a Russian nobleman who continued to dream of his extreme fear of wolves. It was his research on this case that allowed him to build his theories on child sexuality and the Oedipus Complex.

The Turks, Mongolians, Chinese, Japanese and many other cultures saw the strength, cunning and fighting prowess of the wolf as real and necessary to their culture.

The Buddha's Nose

Apollo saw the wolf as a great hero warrior and ancestor. It is said that both Zeus and Osiris took the shape of the wolf to defend against nature's droughts and man's evilness.

Most esotericists will agree that the wolf is the personification of the Conductor of the Soul... the PSYCHOPOMP. When the image of the wolf penetrates our dreamlife it is the Psychopomp that stands ready to communicate between our High and Low Selves. He is the glue of spiritual congruency. For many of us the road to enlightenment may well be through the forces of the Wolf.

Toni could certainly tell you about the powers of the wolf...if you get the chance she'll share a true story or two, but don't be wearing socks when she does.

Chapter Twenty-Two - Dope-A-Rope

I have had two main heroes in my life, both because they were honest and true men with immense senses of self. Each in his own way provided me with (and still do) an understanding and appreciation for the depth of the human spirit.

Cassius Clay/Muhammad Ali was the greatest boxer I ever saw either in person or on film. He continued to prove conclusively that he was 'the best' and it seemed that each time he uttered the "I AM THE BEST" mantra, sure enough it turned out to be that he was. He believed in himself over all else because he knew who and what he was....he was truly authentic. He was a missionary of good against a plethora of evil as he graphically showed in his two fights with convicted criminal and bully standover man Sonny Liston, so called the 'baddest man in town.' He went on from those fights to become a god to many and an inspiration to thousands upon thousands world wide, including me. First of all he was a man and secondly he was a champion fighter for years. He was powerful, proud and fearless. But I found out first hand that he was something else: he was a humanist and a benefactor.

The Buddha's Nose

A long time ago I was giving a series of lectures in Manila to the senior staff of the largest Life Insurance Company in the country and about half way through the series I had a day off for some R and R. That afternoon I decided to rent a car and drive around the town a bit just to see the sights. Before I knew it I was on the outskirts of the city and the demographics had well and truly changed. All around me was intense poverty. It made me sad and thankful at the same time.

Just then I glanced over to my right and there in front of me was the name ALI on some kind of building. I couldn't see the first name as it was hidden from my view but I decided to check it out. Eventually I was able to turn around, cross the street and backtrack till I found the entrance to a parking lot in front of a low slung yellow coloured building of questionable construction but in surprisingly good repair given where it was situated. The name MUHAMMAD ALI in big brash letters, like the champ himself, I thought, was printed imposingly across the front. I parked and went in with some kind of nervousness as to what would happen to me next.

It was a huge boxing gym with all of the up to date equipment you would expect to find in any current gym of its kind. I was amazed. Here in the middle of this downtrodden part of the city was a beacon of class and potential. Dozens of young people, and a few not so, were doing their thing. The four rings were fully in use, so were the bags and skipping ropes as well as the weight section ...the joint was jumpin.'

The Buddha's Nose

The Manager saw me come in and made a beeline to me. Unfortunately I can't recall his name but he was a retired pro boxer and had been assigned by Ali to run the gym. I spent almost an hour with the man and in that time I learned a great deal more about my hero. Ali had funded the entire operation, as he had done in other areas of the world, and his whole purpose was not to first find another champion or two... it was first to offer kids a chance at a better life. I left there loving him even more!

His mental strength at refusing to become inducted into the Vietnam war and the troubles and enormous money that he lost with his rebellion, the fact that his only livelihood was stripped away from him with no thought to or for his future, his decision to become a Muslim against all kinds of threats to him and his family, his constant love of people and his belief in himself all helped make him the man he is today, even though he suffers bravely with Parkinson disease. I am sure that those who care for him now suffer deeply along with him, as do his fans like me.

I want to focus now on just one small section of Ali's career. It was his fight with George Foreman. At the time George was a mean and miserable big bastard very much like Sonny Liston had been a few years earlier but even larger and meaner. He was also an amazing fighter who knocked out all before him and showed no mercy. When the match was first announced, very few people who knew the fight game gave Ali any chance at all. The odds were astronomical that he would lose and that George would knock him out and into oblivion (that's a small town in South Africa).

The Buddha's Nose

But Ali had a plan. It was called ROPE A DOPE. The plan worked and to the surprise and shock of most of us who thought he would be literally killed he knocked George out ...Georgie boy paid the visit to oblivion instead. By the way, soon after that fight George changed his ways and today is a well respected and loved minister of the faith, father of umpteen boys, each named George, and a protector of kids.

Ali's plan was to work himself into a corner of the ring on the ropes and allow George to shuffle in and throw his enormous lefts and rights into Ali's body. Eventually the thunderous shots would slow down and lose their power as George became tired, and then Ali would attack. It happened exactly that way.

Winston Churchill is my other hero. Here was a guy who usually slept in his clothes, smoked incredibly foul-smelling cigars according to those who knew him well, was a first class, world class boozer and undoubtedly saved the free world while he was at it. I'm sure that if it had not been for Winston's political ability and incredible mind I would not be free to write this today, and probably you wouldn't be free to read it. I think that while he didn't shoot a bullet or pour a glass of poison it was Winston's strength that ultimately led to Adolph's demise.

During his life Winston was known as a word merchant, he loved the English language and protected its veracity whenever he could. Grammar was a particular thing with him. He felt that people who spoke bad grammar had little education and therefore did not possess disciplined minds. But he was also an advocate of the concept that says 'rules are meant to be broken.' He suffered fools badly and was often quick to anger when he saw stupidity or lack of logic. Somewhere along the line he adopted a particular 'breaking of the rules' that allowed him to alter grammar briefly to attend to his anger or frustration most effectively.

When that emotion would attack him he would express the depth of his negativity on the subject by loudly proclaiming: 'UP WITH WHICH I WILL NOT PUT.' Today, we use that complete expression when it's necessary but more often we tend to just express our feelings with a 'that's a Churchill', or 'that's a Winston' and the message gets through loud and clear to the listener - if they know whence it comes.

Back to Rope-a-Dope and more importantly to my title of this chapter, Dope-A-Rope. I used to smoke some joints the thickness of a skipping rope, hence the title. It all began in the summer of 1969 in Woodland Hills, California and it lasted until the winter of 1999 in Newcastle, New South Wales. That summer friends introduced me to the wonderful experiences of 'losing control,' loving the world, enlightening my love of all things living or dead and the magnificent force of the 'munchies.' So, for thirty years of my life I suffered from an addiction so lethal that I was disconnected from the realities of life most of the time. No matter what country I was residing in I was under the hypnotic influence of the ever-encompassing darkening cloud of Mary Jane.

Naturally I didn't see it as 'dark,' to me it was simply pleasant, shooed the willies away and provided me with an outlet for social exposure. Tensions were relieved, troubles were minimised and nothing seemed to be as important as it should have been. Quite simply I was living a lie!

With the exception of trying mushroom once in Toronto (a full day experience that left me stunned, confused and unimpressed) I never felt the need or the pull to reach for anything higher than grass. In retrospect I see that as an absolute blessing.

My experiences in later years with young patients who had become schizoid showed me clearly the impaling results the weed could have on the out of balance, unsuspecting or the unprepared...especially those who chose to travel to India to 'find' themselves. They found themselves alright, at the bottom of a sickly, dirty, smoky bong sucking away their remaining sense of self and positive future while destroying their very essence of authenticity. Too bad!

Today, of course, more and more countries are approving the legal use of the drug. It certainly does have some benefit as a pain relief medicine, but its overuse must be severely concerning.

Fast Eddie had a favourite saying that he used often 'everything in moderation.' Basically I suspect he was right, so were the Buddhists. The problem is knowing when and how to 'moderate.'

Since 1969 I have given up on the things that I saw as immoderate...coffee, tea, cigarettes, wheat and grass. The only one that still pulls on me some times is the latter.

The Buddha's Nose

Irving Says

We are often addicted to grass and don't even know **it.** We just really like **it,** we enjoy **it**, **it** makes us laugh, **it** makes us feel better, **it** helps us sleep, **it** calms us down, **it** turns us on, **it** turns us off, **it** helps us dig music, **it** helps us tolerate people, **it** has a social value, **it** makes us more creative, **it** takes away our pain, **it** sets us free, **it** doesn't cost too much, **it** is easy to get.

It has all kinds of excuses for **its** use in our lives but one thing is for sure: ***it disconnects us from reality***. To that extent **it** can easily be perceived as purely a self-hypnotic, self-administered religion. But there's something strange about paying homage to a fast growing weed and then having some kind of a shit-fit when we run out of supply. 'Moderation' has come and gone then!

Sometimes we might disguise addiction by using the word **habit** in its place, but if we fool ourselves that way then we are only fooling a FOOL.

1. Define for yourself the word 'addiction' and write it down where you can see it clearly.

2. Adhering to your own definition make a list of addictions that are in your life now and beside each one give a rating from one to 5, five being the highest (you should pardon the pun).

3. For those rated three or more think about what it will take to get rid of them altogether and make an appropriate note beside them.

4. Start the process now!

5. *Good Luck, nothing really worthwhile ever comes to us easily, except maybe Lotto*

Chapter Twenty-Three - Dear Reader

This book is about imperfections. Mine. Writing it has been an experience for sure. Releasing some of those secrets from the past has been relieving, frightening and insightful....what if you don't like me now? What if you don't believe me? What if you think I've been a fool to let my guard down? What if you think I'm just putting you on? And, worst of all, what if you just don't give a damn about the book or what its intentions were or are. That would be the killer for me. I wrote this with a purpose in mind as outlined at the very beginning.....to help men deal with their difficulties today. Replaying scenes that were created in the past without resolution are terrible foes and seem to be unbeatable, but you can achieve more and lasting peace by confronting your Dweller.

At the same time I think there may be women who might read this to learn more about their men, including their husbands, ex-husbands, fathers and grandfathers. I hope so.

At the age of 82 I have had a full and exciting life, lived in many cities around the world, travelled to many more; had wives, kids, money, prestige, sorrow, happiness, pain, fear, indecision, indiscretion- but maybe more of this and less of that.

Now I have a true love with Toni, good health for both of us, a few bucks in the bank, a comfortable Darwin home filled with honesty and an anxious outlook for what tomorrow brings. I have two beautiful, blue-eyed Ragdoll cats whom I adore, a good car, a red scooter, a bank, gym, dentist, doctor, hospital and shopping centre all no more than five minutes away and just 60 seconds to the beach. I need nothing and have everything.

I feel I've paid my dues, like most of us do I suppose.

And now my goal is to help you help yourself perhaps. There is nothing written here that is not accurate or honest. Where there is a workshop you can rest assured that it has been road tested many times. When there is a personal philosophy expressed by me it's as good as gold. That sounds a bit arrogant, which I don't mean to imply, I mean I've worked on it and it works for me. When I mention other people's philosophies I can only stand by what I have personally experienced about them as I studied their ways and means.

Years ago, no matter what house he was living in at the time, my Dad had a saying attached to the back of his den's toilet door:

Too soon ve git olde und too late ve git schmart

Fast Eddie taught me a lot of things in my life but nothing more profound than that. The older I got, the more I understood the message.

The Buddha's Nose

Hmm, I think I can hear the Fat Lady singing.........
I wish you Light, Love and Power

Regards
Ted

St Jeanne d'Arc

Coming Soon.....

My next book, HEALER! will be ready before long.

Here's a sample:

Chapter One

The sun's harsh rays streamed down from directly overhead as he began to slowly rein in his huge glistening pure white stallion. They had ridden together since early sun-up and most of the time it was at a gallop as they went from town to town visiting the aged, sick, feeble and disabled, healing where possible and providing mental sustenance to all who came within his aura.

Today was May the eighth in the year 524 B.C., his 35th birthday, and very early this morning when he left his beautiful wife and young son still sleeping he had promised them last night that he would return before dark today to enjoy the party that was planned for him. As a Prince, Siddhartha Gautama knew that this was an important day for others to share with him.

As they came over a hill, there below them was a serene picture of tranquillity, a place he knew was meant for them, a place to rest and tether before returning home. He spotted a large majestic tree sitting imposingly beside a crystal clear pool of the bluest of blue water. The draw was immediate.

He dismounted and left the horse to fend for itself at the water's edge while he walked slowly but purposefully toward the beckoning of the tree and the shade it offered.

As he made himself comfortable under the cover of the Bodhi tree he thought of his father, the King, and how he had wanted so much for his son to become the great world ruler, as the Brahmans had suggested would be the case when he was born. But somehow he knew that his father would not be disappointed in him and his life, although it would not be what had been planned.

Gautama had well prepared himself for what was to come. Over the years he had studied, served and meditated on all matters metaphysical under the highest quality of teachers of the realm and knew within himself that there was a transformation about to occur ....he could feel it coming, it seemed to be bubbling just below the surface of his being. He noticed he was in a state of numinousness now, as he began to doze.

Then, sleep.

The dream was alive with energy and meaning. It was majestic. It was real. It was both a dream and a vision. It was direction and purpose. It was overwhelming.

He awoke a new man, a Buddha, a supremely enlightened teacher. He knew what he had to do now, how many lives he had had and how many were to come before he left the planet, he knew he would live to the age of 80 in this incarnation, he knew he could project himself anywhere at any time, he knew he must teach and heal and that he must teach healing. He was a Healer!

His magnificent steed stood quietly beside him also under the shade lazily swishing his tail to frighten away the flies. The horse seemed to know.

The Buddha stood up, swaying slightly but strengthening quickly.

He mounted and patted the horse on the neck lovingly before saying to him out loud, "Well, old friend, it's time to go. I think we're going to have some kind of dinner tonight, don't you?"..........

* * *

Since his death in 489 B.C. the Buddha had lived many productive and important lives but this one would challenge his ability as a teacher of the modern day, using the language of the modern day. He welcomed what he knew was coming.

It began snowing heavily in the middle hours of the morning of December 20th 2015. The flakes that wafted slowly down to earth were like millions of individual micro-thin white velvet pieces of angel dust, each landing softly in a given spot and there settling quickly into their new home, one on top of the other.

By early evening the entire city was covered inches deep by the glorious, crisp, heaven-sent doona. The air was cold, but brisk and clean. It was the kind of night approaching that brought with it a peculiar kind of joy that most people shared when they were able to walk in and on it. And to experience the sensation of the crunching under foot, while breathing in deeply the almost hypnotising effects of the purest of air, made it seem as though each person possessed their own private vacuum of special space dedicated to the acknowledgement of the beauty of Mother Nature.

The usual sounds of the busy metropolis going about its own collective, hectic existence were hushed and dampened by the still-falling snow, unyielding.

The Buddha glanced at the watch on his wrist. Not quite seven, still an hour to go.

This was his first time in Toronto and he was enjoying the experience, as he always did when he visited a place initially. It was metropolitan.

He had thoroughly assessed the city's vibes on his half hour walk from the hotel to the auditorium. His awareness levels were at their peaks as he "melted" into the environment. Nothing was missed...not the exquisite churches, not the ornate office buildings, nor the demeanour of the passing pedestrians, the types of cars that traversed their ways through the reduced visibility and the slippery conditions of the night, not the hushed sound of the underground beneath his feet as it zipped by him, not the various types of outstanding architecture that were presented to his senses and not the soft north winds that breezed unfettered from a cold but still imposing Lake Ontario.

He stuck out one of his gloved hands and caught a few of the white velvet creatures of creation as they fell by him. He tasted a few inquisitively and then breathed deeply and felt an immediate sensation of peace and tranquility overcome him. The feeling was similar to that which came with a powerful meditation. It was as if he had control of two separate universes, one that was physical and visible, and the other which was neither.

"A very Christian and Catholic city with powerful cross cultures," he mused to himself as he approached his destination. "Interesting that the fates would have it that I should spend my first trip to this beautiful city just five days before Christmas," he noted almost off-handedly.

He stood out front of the auditorium now and carefully surveyed it. Six steps up to the large ornately carved door. Carefully constructed and placed in such a position as to not be considered pretentious or over-bearing within the confines of the Central Business District, it appeared to beckon warmly to those that would notice it, similar to the type of attraction that fine churches or synagogues present to those who are in tune with them.

He paused and painted the building with his White Light of Protection.

Then, using his Astral Projection technique, he entered the classroom inside, reviewed it carefully noting the set-up and air conditioning, while implanting his attitude and energy, which he would meet and don when he physically entered the room later.

Before long, he knew, he would actually be teaching Astral Projection and Attitude Implanting to many excited and interested students.................................

www.ingramcontent.com/pod-product-compliance
Lightning Source LLC
Chambersburg PA
CBHW072127270326
41931CB00010B/1690